Sandra Polley's

Knitted Toys

Sandra Polley's
Knitted Toys

Arbour House Publishing
www.arbourhousepublishing.com

First Published in 2010 by
Arbour House Publishing
Southport, UK
www.arbourhousepublishing.com

Editor: Susan Crawford
Photography: Susan Crawford & Charlie Moon
Illustration & Design: Gavin Crawford

British Library Cataloguing-in-Publication Data
A catalogue record for this book is available from the British Library

ISBN 978-0-9556206-4-5

Printed and bound in the UK

This book can be purchased directly from
www.arbourhousepublishing.com

Contents

Introduction

I hope if you are reading this it is because you love knitting and especially knitted toys. Being a bit lazy, I like a hobby that I can do sitting on my sofa. I might spread out a bit but when I've had enough it only takes a few minutes to put it all in a little bag. That's the great thing about knitting toys, its relaxing, not much mess, doesn't take too long and hopefully there's something at the end of it that someone will actually want.

I have always loved craftwork, especially toy making. There is a feeling of creating a life, a little character, from just scraps of yarn or fabric, which if loved by a child will be given a name and a personality, perhaps even quite a long life.

So I have enjoyed making all of these different characters. Some were easier than others to design, it was difficult deciding how far to go with the dog hand puppets and I thought I would never get the Meerkat pattern finished!

As with many people though, I adore Meerkats and just had to make one. I didn't want to give them the indignity of too many clothes so they have only what they can find on their travels around the desert. I hope they will appeal to both adults and children. They can be made smaller than the two sizes given by adjusting yarn and knitting needles. I have even made some very small ones as gifts for adult Meerkat lovers using 3 ply yarn and 2mm needles.

The idea for the hand puppets was a combination of my love of dogs, wanting to make something for interacting play with my Grandson Jack and memories of 'Spit the dog' (a badly behaved hand puppet from 1980s children's TV). The puppets can be made in two sizes so anyone can be a naughty dog. They can pick things up in their mouths and nibble little fingers! All of which cannot fail to amuse a small child.

Before you begin to knit any of the patterns, do take a few minutes to read the general instructions. Much of it you may already know but it will help to understand some of my peculiarities in toy making and also saves space by my not having to repeat things for every pattern.

All of the patterns are easy to follow, with no complicated stitches or designs and many can be made from quite small amounts of yarn. The clothes have also been kept to a simple design and are quick and easy to knit. The reindeer and elves are perfect for decorating the Christmas tree and the little dolls and bears can be quickly made for last minute gifts or stocking fillers.

I hope you enjoy making these little characters and that they are loved by children young and old.

I especially hope that you find knitting one relaxing, that you like your finished toy and look forward to making another one!

Sandra Polley

Materials

Yarn

All the yarn I used for the toys in this book was relatively cheap and would be quite easy to find, especially nowadays with online shopping so much easier. So many other shops sell yarn and haberdashery items now. There is even a nice selection in my local chemist!

Yarn with a high wool content is not really suitable for these small toys, other than perhaps Jim and the baby gift bears. The edges of the knitted pieces curl in too much and make the projects, especially the small ones difficult to sew up.

Sewing thread

You will need some embroidery thread for darning noses, mostly black or brown. You could use yarn but it would be a bit thick for most of the toys.

You will also need household sewing thread for attaching press fasteners and buttons and some black extra strong thread for sewing on bead eyes. I also use it for making mouse whiskers.

Knitting needles

There aren't many different sizes of knitting needles used in this book. Most of the double knitting projects are knitted with 3mm needles. I have used the size needle I thought the most appropriate but if you know that your knitting tension is too tight or too loose you can use a size larger or smaller needles as appropriate.

Try to get shortish needles if you can as none of the knitted pieces have long rows and long needles might get in the way.

Stuffing

Years ago, Teddy Bears were stuffed with straw, wood, wool, kapok etc and during the war years, old bits of rags and clothes. Nowadays you can buy good quality toy filling from haberdashers and craft shops. This stuffing is clean, light, relatively cheap and easy to use. It will also have been tested for fire resistance. Another good source of stuffing can be found in new polyester quilts and pillows. They are also inexpensive if you buy one from a supermarket and they will also have a safety standard mark which means the stuffing will be fire resistant. Foam chips are not any good for making small toys, they will make them lumpy and they are very difficult and messy to use.

Sewing needles

Needles for sewing knitted pieces together have a blunt point to prevent the yarn splitting and a large eye to thread the thick yarn through. They are generally called 'tapestry', 'yarn' or 'knitters' needles and they are available in many different sizes. A medium size, either No. 18 or 20 is about right for sewing up double knitting and 4 ply toys. You will also need a household sewing needle for darning facial features, attaching press fasteners and a few other little bits.

Eyes

Some of the eyes for these toys are embroidered. These are the safest eyes for young children. Jim, Oscar, Nipper and Elliot have plastic safety eyes. As they are a medium size they are safe for older children because they are not small enough to slip out of the stitches and if fixed in properly, they are almost impossible to pull out. The miniature bear and the Meerkats have very small bead eyes. They look very effective but must not be used for toys intended for small children.

Forceps or Tweezers

These are very useful pieces of equipment and are essential when making the miniature bear. They will help to turn the finished pieces out the right way after sewing up and they will grip and stuff small amounts of stuffing into all the tiny spaces. Veterinary forceps are better than tweezers as they are slightly curved and have a locking ratchet. If you visit your local Veterinary centre, they might be willing to order you a pair. Mine were about £6.00 and I have had them over 9 years now.

Pins

You should only use the coloured plastic headed pins for knitted toys as they can be easily seen and are not so likely to slip through and get lost in your knitting. The black headed ones are also very useful for trying out eye positions.

I have to be very careful with pins and needles when my Grandson or Border Terrier are around. Jack hasn't yet trod on one but I found the lunatic dog chewing a pin the other day!

Pencil

A pencil is useful for marking where you are on the pattern as you go along or if you get disturbed. You can then erase the marks afterwards.

Scissors

A sharp pair of embroidery scissors are best to snip off threads. My favourites are the little stainless steel, plastic handled ones you often see in supermarkets. You will also need a larger pair of scissors to cut some wadding for Elliot and Nipper, the hand puppets.

Buttons and beads

Many craft suppliers sell tiny buttons. Small beads also make nice buttons for miniature toys. I used gold beads for the Elf and Leprechaun jackets. Larger, household buttons make very good joints for toys for older children or adults. I like the quirky look of them on the outside of the limbs as with the Christmas Reindeer.

There are a few projects in the book which require beads and sequins. Lots of pretty beads can be found in craft shops, car boot sales and charity shops. Sequins are sold in haberdashery shops and market places.

Tape measure

Although most of the instructions state the amount of rows to knit, there are occasionally pieces of work to measure.

Safety

Most of the rules governing safety when making and giving knitted toys to children are really just common sense. Obviously, scissors, needles and pins should not be left lying around when there are young children about, limbs should be sewn on securely and any loose threads darned into the toys out of sight. We all know that young children should not be given toys with tiny parts which can be pulled off and swallowed*. I have to say all this though and you must remember to mention it if you make any of these bears for fundraising events.

* Do not use beads, buttons or detachable eyes on toys or teddies intended for babies or children under 3 years of age, as they may cause a choking hazard if swallowed.

General Instructions

Needle sizes

mm	US	UK
5	8	6
4½	7	7
4	6	8
3¼	4	10
3	3	11
2¾	2	12
2¼	1	13

Weight conversion

To convert grammes to ounces use:
oz = g × 0.0352

Abbreviations

St	Stitch
St st	Stocking stitch – 1 row knit, 1 row purl
G. st	Garter stitch – every row knit
K	Knit
P	Purl
Dec	Decrease, by knitting/purling 2 stitches together
Inc	Increase, by knitting/purling into the front and back of a stitch
m1	Make 1 – make a stitch by knitting into back of loop before next stitch
Beg.	Beginning
Tog	Together
Alt.	Alternate
RS	Right side of work
WS	Wrong side of work
Rib	K1, P1, across row
Sl 1	Slip next stitch
yfwd	Yarn forward
Rep	Repeat
Cont	Continue
foll.	Following

Stitches used

Stocking stitch

All of the toys are knitted in stocking stitch. Duncan is sewn up with purl sides together, which when turned right way out becomes reverse stocking stitch.

Garter stitch

Some of the clothes and accessories are knitted in garter stitch, which means every row is knitted.

Single rib

All of the rib in this book is single rib, which is knit 1, purl 1 to end of row, repeated on an even number of stitches. For example:
First row: K1, P1, K1, P1.
Repeat first row until required length.

There are also a few simple patterns used for clothes, these are explained in the project instructions.

Brackets

When instructions are given in brackets it means they are to be repeated by the amount of times stated.

Using pins

When pinning small pieces of work together, place the pins in at right angles to the seam, this takes up less room and keeps the sharp point of the pins out of the way.

Using markers

Some of the patterns contain instructions to place markers. This is to help with sewing up the pieces. A couple of the projects, such as the hand puppets would be quite complicated to sew up without them. The easiest way to do this is to have a yarn needle threaded with a long length of yarn of a different shade to the one you are using. Wherever you need to put a marker, make a couple of little stitches around 1 knitted stitch and then snip off close to your work. You can either carefully pull out the markers later after sewing up or remove them as you get to them.

Backstitch

This is a good stitch to use when you need a strong neat line or seam, such as the inside edge of Harriet bear's day bed.

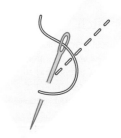

Backstitch

Running stitch

This one isn't used very much as it isn't very strong. It is ok for temporary holding when the piece is going to be sewn again at some point.

Running stitch

Oversew stitch

This stitch is very easy and the best way to sew up all the little clothes. It is worked on the wrong side, with right sides together. Take very small stitches from both edges of work, one from each row and work from back to front and then over to the back again for each stitch.

Oversew Stitch

Ladderstitch

This is the best way to close a seam on the right side of your toy after stuffing it. Knot a length of thread and secure it at the edge of the opening in the seam. Take small stitches either side of the open seam, gently pulling the seam closed every three or four stitches to the end. Secure with a couple more stitches.

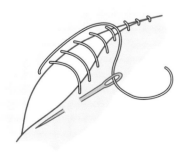

Ladderstitch

Darning in threads

Apart from the long thread left at the top of the miniature bears' ears and maybe one or two other places, it is easier to rethread and darn all the loose threads into the edge or back of your work and trim them before sewing up. You might think that they are useful to sew up with but they only get in the way and are usually too short to use anyway.

Casting off

You will see that when casting off at the top of the limbs and some other places, the instructions say either to slip the first stitch or knit 2 together at each end of the row at the same time. This is to help smooth out the shaped edges of the seams and is quite easy to do. Cast off in the usual way but either slip the first stitch on to the right needle without knitting it, or knit 2 together, cast off to the last 2 stitches, knit 2 together and cast off last stitch.

Increasing and Decreasing

There are only two ways to increase or decrease throughout the book. Some of the projects, such as waistcoats and some head gussets need a smooth edge so it is better to increase or decrease 1 stitch in from the edge for example:-

Decrease: K1, K2 tog, K to last 3 sts, K2 tog, K1.
   or
Increase: Inc 1, K to last 2 sts, inc 1, K1.

But you don't want any shaping to show on some of the seams, such as tiny doll faces or some of the clothes so it is better to knit 2 edge stitches together for decreasing or knit twice in the first and last stitch for increasing. Instructions for which to use are given in the pattern.

Tension

Your tension is not too important for most of the toys because it doesn't really matter if your bear or toy comes out a little bit bigger or smaller than the finished size given. If you know that you are a very loose knitter then use a size smaller needles, or use larger needles if you knit tightly.

It is important though, to use the same thickness of yarn for the clothes as used for the toy, otherwise they might not fit. Some double knitting or 4 ply yarns are thicker than others and this will make a difference to the finished size.

Pressing

Not many of the toy pieces need pressing. As most are sewn up with right sides together, the edges usually come together nicely.

One exception is the miniature bear Duncan. His knitted pieces will need a good press as they are to be sewn up with purl sides together to make a reverse stocking stitch bear. Pin them out, wrong side facing to a flat pad or the ironing board and cover them with a damp cloth to press with a warm iron.

Sewing up the pieces

Always take your time sewing up the pieces and try to work in good light, daylight if possible. If you do work in the evening and need extra light there are some very good halogen lamps about now.

We all have our way of doing things, I always knot the end of any thread that I am sewing up with.

Stuffing

As with all soft toys, how you stuff them will directly affect the finished appearance. It is important to stuff firmly but without stretching the knitting out of place. Always stuff well down into the extremities such as the nose and paws or hands first and mould into shape as you go along. A pair of forceps or tweezers are very useful for stuffing the smaller toys, especially the miniatures. If you are thread-jointing a finished bear, put plenty of stuffing in the body as the jointing will pull it in. The amount of stuffing needed for each toy will vary depending on knitting tension and individual taste, therefore requirements given for each pattern are approximate.

Aftercare

Most of the toys can be washed by hand and spun inside a pillowcase. The larger ones will probably need to be dried outside on a warm day to make sure they are dry right through.

Sewing faces

As mentioned in the materials section, it is best to embroider facial features with embroidery thread rather than yarn, which is usually too thick. For the little Ted's in this book, a small neat triangle is sewn horizontally.

With the miniature dolls I think you would agree that 'less is more' so to speak. Use only one or two strands at a time for the eyes (usually brown rather than black). The black headed pins are ideal for trying out eye positions for all the toys. Make one tiny stitch and then sew two or three more exactly on top. On some of the dolls I have made 2 tiny stitches on each eye to make eyelashes.

Although the mouth itself is only two or three stitches, how you place it will have a big impact on your toys face and you may have to experiment a bit before you get the look you want. For the nose you could either sew two tiny stitches in brown or make a couple of dots with a brown felt tip pen.

Some ideas are given here which may be of help to choose your toy's personality.

Miniature doll face
Keep the features very small, with 1 tiny stitch sewn over and over a few times for the eyes

How you space the eyes on a bear can make him look young or older, relaxed or puzzled

How much yarn do I need?

For many of the patterns I haven't stated how much yarn or stuffing you will need. For so many little toys, clothes and accessories, it would take forever to work it out and would not be very accurate either. A lot of it is down to common sense really. If it states embroidery thread for a miniature dolls eyes and you have more than a few centimetres then you have plenty. You can usually look at an oddment of yarn and guess whether there is enough for a tiny dolls cardigan or Meerkat waistcoat. Having said that, I have tried to estimate the amount needed wherever I can.

Workshops

Quite often with knitted toys just a few variations in colour, yarn and needles size can produce completely different looking toys. One example is how with a change of colour, longer legs and a set of antlers, Milly the little white dog became a Christmas Reindeer. There are half a dozen or so toys throughout this book, which have been adapted from the one before it. I call these 'workshop' patterns and they are clearly identified throughout the book.

After making a few toys you will probably see all sorts of variations that can be made by adapting the patterns to make your own unique toys.

Toys

Hannah and Grace

Hannah wears a traditional long sleeved dress while Grace likes her up to date pink and white outfit.
Both dolls and clothes are quickly knitted in stocking stitch.

Height

Approximately 30cm (11¾ in)

Materials

- 1 × 50g ball DK yarn in flesh pink for Hannah and brown for Grace.
- 1 × 25g ball each of black and yellow DK yarn for hair.
- 1 × 50g ball DK yarn in light blue for dress.
- Oddments of DK yarn in white, pink and dark red for rest of clothes.
- Length of medium blue yarn or embroidery thread for Hannah's eyes.
- 1 pair each of 3mm and 3¼mm knitting needles.
- Black, brown and white sewing thread.
- Wool needle and small sewing needle.
- Polyester stuffing.
- 4 small white beads for decorating dress and jumper.
  Do not use for young children
- 6 small press fasteners for dress and jumper.
- Thin ribbon in red and pink for hair.

Head and Body

With 3mm needles and body colour of choice, cast on 37 sts.
Row 1: K2, (inc1, K3) to last 3 sts, inc 1, K2 (46 sts).
St st 9 rows, ending on a P row.

To shape bottom

Dec 1 st at each end of next and 3 foll. alt rows (38 sts).
St st 19 rows, ending on a P row.

To shape shoulders

Next row: K8, K2 tog twice, K14, K2 tog twice, K8 (34 sts).
Next row: P.
Next row: K7, K2 tog twice, K12, K2 tog twice, K7 (30 sts).
Next row: P.
Next row: K6, K2 tog twice, K10, K2 tog twice, K6 (26 sts).
St st 3 rows.

To shape head

Next row: K2, inc 1, K2, inc in every st until 5 sts remain, K2, inc 1, K2 (44 sts).
St st 9 row, ending on a P row.
Next row: K10, K2 tog twice, K16, K2 tog twice, K10 (40 sts).
St st 13 rows, ending on a P row.
Next row: K2 tog across row (20 sts).
Next row: P2 tog across row (10 sts).
Break yarn and thread through remaining sts, pull up tight and fasten off, leaving a long thread to sew up head and body with.

Arms – make 2

To shape hands

With 3mm needles and body colour, cast on 8 sts.
First row: Inc 1, K2, inc in next 2 sts, K2, inc 1 (12 sts).
Next row: P.
Inc 1 st at each end of next and following alt row (16 sts).
Next row: P.
Dec 1 st at each end of next and foll. alt row (12 sts).
St st 7 rows, ending on a P row.
Next row: Inc 1, K to last 2 sts, inc 1, K1 (14 sts).
St st 15 rows, ending on a P row.
Cast off, knitting 2 sts tog at each end of row at same time.

Legs – make 2

To shape feet

With 3mm needles and white, cast on 9 sts.
First row: Inc in every st (18 sts).
Next row: P.
Next row: K1, inc in every st until last st, K1 (34 sts).
St st 3 rows.
Next row: K7, K2 tog 10 times, K7 (24 sts).
Next row: P.
Next row: K7, K2 tog 5 times, K7 (19 sts).
Next row: P.
Next row: K7, K2 tog 3 times, K6 (16 sts).
Next row: P7, P2 tog, P7 (15 sts).
Next row: K7, inc 1, K7 (16 sts).
St st 2 rows.
G. st 3 rows.
Change to body colour and starting with a K row, st st 10 rows, ending on a P row.
Inc 1 st at each end of next and following 10th row (20 sts).
St st 9 rows. Cast off.

General Notes

Start all pieces with a K row unless otherwise stated. After working each piece, neaten by darning the loose threads into the back of your work or into the body pieces out of sight, whichever is relevant.

To ensure that clothes fit well, try to keep to the same thickness of DK yarn for both the doll and the clothes wherever possible. Both dolls are the same.

To make up doll

Sew up all body pieces with right sides tog.

Body and Head

With right sides tog, fold lengthways and sew up seam from top of head to bottom cast on edge with appropriate coloured yarn, leaving a gap in the back for turning and stuffing. The seam lies at the centre back of the doll. Turn right side out and stuff the head and shoulders carefully, filling out the cheeks and moulding into shape as you go. Tie a length of body coloured yarn around the neck, pull up tightly and fasten off. Stuff the rest of the body, pushing more stuffing into the shoulders but leave the bottom few cms unstuffed for now. Tease out the chin and cheeks with your wool/tapestry needle, digging quite deeply to pull the stuffing forward.

Ears – Optional

(they will not show much with long hair)
With body coloured yarn and dolls face uppermost, take a pinch of knitting either side and about halfway up the head (on cheek shaping if you can see it) and backstitch about 2 or 3 sts through both layers down towards the neck. Secure with a couple more sts and fasten off.

Legs

Fold lengthways and sew up from bottom cast on edge to top, turn right way out and stuff to within 1cm (½ in) of the top. Make sure stuffing is pushed well down into the toes, moulding into shape as you go. With the seam lying at centre back, press the tops closed and oversew. Insert and sandwich the top of the legs just inside the base of the body, adjacent to the body sides and with a small gap between them. Backstitch through all layers. Finish stuffing the body through gap left at back, pushing plenty of stuffing into the bottom and close the seam.

Arms

With right sides tog, fold each arm lengthways and sew up seam leaving tops open. Turn out and stuff but leave the top 2cm (¾ in) without stuffing. Flatten the top of the arms with the seam lying at centre back. Oversew closed and sew tops of arms to body under shoulder shaping.

Hair

Fringe

Cut 20 lengths of hair coloured yarn, about 15cm (6 in) long. Lay bunch of threads across top of head from front to back so that the centre of bunch lies on the crown. Backstitch in place. Place 2 pins on forehead, 5cm (2 in) apart and 1cm (½ in) down from crown. Pull all threads forward, fan them out and with another length of yarn, back st the fringe in place between the pins. Trim fringe to about 4cm (1½ in).

Cut 60 × 30cm (12 in) lengths of yarn. Working with 4 or 5 pieces at a time, back st the centre of the yarn lengths to the seam line at the back of the head, starting 1cm (½ in) up from the neck and finishing just over the fringe sewing line.

To make sure that the hair is shared out evenly, you could roughly tack into position first before sewing on neatly. You can add a few more lengths if there are any gaps but too many will make the finished hair bunches very thick. Gather each side of hair, tie into bunches and secure to head with 2 or 3 sts midway between top and bottom of head. Trim neatly and tie on ribbon.

Face

Hannah

Take a length of blue yarn and carefully split the threads apart. With 2 threads, darn the eyes to a round shape, just higher than halfway between the chin and the hairline and 2½cm (1 in) apart. Split a length of white yarn and using 2 threads, backstitch 3 sts into a semicircle above and very close to each pupil *(see diagram a)*.
Note – You do have to be careful splitting and then sewing with the yarn as it becomes quite delicate and easily broken.

Diagram a

Eyelashes

With brown sewing thread, sew 2 tiny stitches outwards from each eye over the whites *(see diagram b)*. With a double length of white sewing thread, sew a tiny st on each eye to bring the eyes to life. Sew 2 little brown sts for eyebrows.

Diagram b

Grace

Using black instead of blue yarn, sew the eyes in a similar way as Hannah's but go over the whites a second time to round off and accentuate a little bit more.

Eyelashes

With black sewing thread, sew 4 tiny sts outwards from pupil to outside of eye *(see diagram c)*. Sew a tiny white st on each eye as for Hannah.

Diagram c

Mouth

Carefully split a length of red yarn and with 2 strands, sew a mouth with 3 small sts halfway between the eyes and chin.

Nose

(If required) – Sew 2 tiny dots in pink lightly lower than midway between eyes and mouth.

Knickers

Made in one piece. Starting and finishing at waistband.

With 3¼mm needles, cast on 21 sts and g.st 3 rows.
Next row: K2, (inc 1, K3) to last 3 sts, inc 1, K2.

Starting with a P row, st st 9 rows.
Next row: K1, K2 tog, K to last 3 sts, K2 tog, K1 (24 sts).
Next row: K1, P2 tog, P to last 3 sts, P2 tog, K1.
Rep last 2 rows until 6 sts remain, ending on a P row.
St st 2 rows.
Increase knitwise at each end of every row until 26 sts, ending on a P row.
St st 8 rows.
Next row: K2, (K2 tog, K3) to last 4 sts, K2 tog, K2 (21 sts).
G. st 3 rows and cast off.

With K sides tog, fold and sew up side seams.

Dress

Skirt

With 3¼mm needles and blue yarn, cast on 104 sts and work in K1, P1 rib for 2 rows.
Starting with a K row, st st 18 rows.
Start of back opening.
Next row: Cast on 2 sts at beg of row.
Next row: K2, P to last 2 sts, K2.
Continue in st st for a further 10 rows, keeping the first and last 2 sts K in every row.
Next row: K3, K2 tog to last 3 sts, K3 (56 sts).
G. st 3 rows.

Bodice

Keeping g. st borders correct, st st 6 rows straight, ending on a P row.

To shape left back

Next row: K13, K2 tog, turn and work on these sts only for now.
Keeping g.st border correct, continue to dec 1 st at inside, armhole edge in next 3 rows (11 sts).
Work 9 rows straight, ending on a K row.

To shape shoulders

Cast off 4 sts at beg of row, work to end
Next row: Cast off 2 sts, break yarn and leave remaining 5 sts on a holder for now.

Front

With right side facing, rejoin yarn, K2 tog, K22, K2 tog, turn and work on these sts only for now.
Dec 1 st at each end of next 3 rows (18 sts).
St st 4 rows straight.

To shape neck

K5, K2 tog, turn.
Next row: P2 tog, P to end.
Next row: K to last 2 sts, K2 tog (4 sts).
Work 3 rows straight and cast off.
With right side facing, leave next 4 sts on a holder for centre front neck, rejoin yarn, K2 tog, K to end.
Complete to match left side of neck, reversing shaping.

To shape right back

With right side facing, rejoin yarn to remaining sts, K2 tog, K to end.
Keeping g.st border correct throughout, dec at armhole edge in next 3 rows (11 sts)
Work 10 rows straight, ending on a P row.

To shape shoulders

Cast off 4 sts at beg of row, work to end.
Next row: Cast off 2 sts, P to end and leave remaining 5 sts on a holder.
With right sides tog, join shoulder seams.

Collar

With 3mm needles, white yarn and right side facing, K the 5 sts from left back holder, pick up and K 8 sts down left neck edge and 2 of the 4 sts from holder at front neck (15 sts).
Turn and work on these sts only for now.
G. st 4 rows, finishing at centre front neck.
Next row: K2 tog, K to end.
Next row: K.
Rep last 2 rows twice (12 sts).
Cast off, knitting 2 sts tog at beg of row.
With right side facing, rejoin yarn and K the 2 remaining sts from front neck holder, pick up and K 8 sts along right neck edge and K 5 sts of right back.
G. st 4 rows, finishing at back edge.
Next row: K to last 2 sts, K2 tog.
Next row: K.
Rep last 2 rows twice (12 sts).
Cast off knitting 2 sts tog at end of row at same time.
With wrong side facing catch collar centre front tog with 1 or 2 sts to neaten. Darn in and snip off loose threads.

Long Sleeves – make 2

With 3mm needles and white yarn, cast on 20 sts and G. st 2 rows.
Change to 3¼mm needles and blue yarn.
Starting with a K row, continue in st st and inc 1 st at each end of next and following 6th row (24 sts).
St st 7 rows straight, ending on a P row.
Mark each end of row.

To shape top

Dec 1 st at each end of next 3 rows (18 sts).
Next row: P.
Dec 1 st at each end of next and following alt row (14 sts).
Cast off, purling 2 sts tog at each end of row at same time.
Join under arm seams from cast on edge

to markers. With right sides together, sew in sleeves.

Sew up back seam of dress from hem to start of back opening. Overlap the g. st borders with the 2 cast on sts on the inside and catch down with a couple of sts. Sew on 3 press fasteners, evenly spaced. Decorate the front of dress with 2 beads or (for younger children) perhaps a couple of French knots.

Jumper

With 3mm needles and white yarn, cast on 56 sts and work in K1, P1 rib for 2 rows.
Change to 3¼mm needles.
Next row: K.
Next row: K2, P to last 2 sts, K2.
Rep last 2 rows 4 times.
Complete as for bodice of dress from start of left back shaping.

Short Sleeves – make 2

With 3mm needles, cast on 20 sts and g. st 2 rows.
Change to 3¼mm needles
Next row: (Inc 1, K5) to last 2 sts, inc 1, K1 (24 sts).
St st 3 rows, ending on a P row.
Mark each end of row.
Shape tops as for long sleeves of dress.

Finish the jumper in the same way as the dress, sewing press fasteners to back and adding a couple of beads or a length of yarn tied into a bow at the front of collar.

Trousers – make 2 pieces

With 3¼mm needles, cast on 30 sts and g. st 2 rows.
Starting with a K row, st st 26 rows. Mark each end of row.

To shape crutch

Cast off 2 sts at beg of next 2 rows.
Next row: Dec 1 st at each end of row
St st 15 rows.
Next row: K2, K2 tog, (K4, K2 tog) to last 2 sts, K2 (20 sts).
G. st 3 rows and cast off.

Pockets – make 2

With 3¼mm needles, cast on 9 sts and st st 9 rows, ending on a K row. K 1 row and cast off.

To make up

With right sides tog, fold each leg length-ways and sew up each inside leg seam from bottom, cast on edge to marker.
Turn one leg right side out and fit into the other, matching crutch seams. Sew from front to back, leaving last 2cm (¾ in) of seam open for back fastening. Sew press fastener on waistband at this opening for easy dressing. Sew pockets in place either side of front seam.

Shoes – make 2

With 3mm needles and red/black yarn, cast on 9 sts.
First row: Inc in every st (18 sts).
Next row: P.
Next row: Inc in every st (36 sts).
St st 3 rows.
Next row: K8, K2 tog 10 times, K8 (26 sts).
Next row: P.
Next row: K7, K2 tog 6 times, K7 (20).
Next row: P.
Next row: K5, turn and P back, slipping the first st.
Next row: K across all sts.
Next row: P5, turn and K back, slipping the first st.
Cast off in P.

With right sides tog, fold the shoe and sew up seam from underfoot to cast off edge at back of ankle. Turn right side out, press out and shape toe of shoes with finger and thumb. With a length of yarn, take a st at centre front of shoe upper, take thread through until there are 2 equal sized 'laces', tie a small bow and trim ends.

Meerkat Family

Apart from the head pieces being a bit fiddly to sew up, these little animals are not as complicated to make as they look. The back legs are knitted into the body to become all one piece. The top of the arms (which are one piece each) are knitted into a row so only the head and tail are sewn on afterwards.

Height
Adults: approximately 24cm (9½in)
Juniors: approximately 18cm (7in)

Materials
- 1 x 50g ball DK yarn in sand colour for each adult Meerkat and about ¾ ball of same for each junior.*
- Oddments of DK yarn for clothes.
- Size 3mm knitting needles.
- 1 pair 5mm beads for adult eyes.
- 1 pair 4mm beads for junior eyes.
- Extra strong black thread.
- Medium brown embroidery thread for eye patches, nose and mouth.
- Brown eyebrow pencil (optional).
- Black embroidery thread for claws.
- Stuffing.

* The Meerkats can also be knitted in a 4 ply yarn. use 2¾mm needles and 3mm beads for eyes.

Pattern Notes
It is important to mark your rows where stated. Sewing up will then become much easier.

Sew up all pieces using a tiny oversew stitch.

Adult Meerkat

Left Arm

Cast on 2 sts.
Inc knitwise in each st (4 sts).
Next row: P.
Next row: Inc 1, K to last 2 sts, inc 1, K1.
St st 3 rows.
Inc as before at each end of next and following alt row (10 sts).
Next row: P.
Next row: Inc 1, K2, K2 tog twice, K1, inc 1, K1.
Next row: P.
Rep last 2 rows twice.

Shape top of arm
Next row: K5, m1, K5.
Next and every foll. alt row for now: P.
Next K row: K5, m1, K1, m1, K5.
Next K row: K5, m1, K3, m1, K5.
Next K row: K5, m1, K5, m1, K5*.
Next row: Cast off 7 sts, P to end (10 sts).
Mark each end of row.
St st 2 rows.
Leave sts on a spare needle for now.

Right arm

Work as left arm to *
Next row: P10, cast off last 7 sts (10 sts).
Break yarn and mark each end of row.
Rejoin yarn and st st 2 rows.
Leave sts on a spare needle for now.

Body, Feet and legs

Cast on 4 sts.
Inc knitwise in each st (8 sts).
Next and every foll. alt row for now: P.
Next K row: K1, inc in every st to last st, K1 (14 sts).

Next K row: K5, K2 tog twice, K5 (12 sts).
Next K row: K4, K2 tog twice, K4 (10 sts).
Next K row: Inc 1, K2, K2 tog twice, K2, inc 1.
Next row: P.
Rep last 2 rows once.
Next row: K4, K2 tog, K4.
Next row: P.
Next row: K2 tog, K2, m1, K1, m1, K2, K2 tog.
Next row: P.
Mark each end of row.

Leave these sts on a holder for now and make another foot the same.

Next row: Cast on 5 sts at beg of row, K until there are 8 sts on right needle, m1, K3, m1, K to end, turn and cast on 6 sts, turn back and K across first 3 sts of other foot, m1, K3, m1, K to end, turn and cast on 5 sts (38 sts).
Mark each end of row.
Next row: P.
Next row: Inc in first st, K7, m1, K5, m1, K4, K2 tog twice, K4, m1, K5, m1, K6, inc 1, K1 (42 sts).
Next row: P.

Bottom shaping
Next row: K7, turn, sl 1, P back.
　　　　　K6, turn, sl 1, P back.
　　　　　K5, turn, sl 1, P back.
Next row: K9, m1, K7, m1, K3, K2 tog twice, K3, m1, K7, m1, K9 (44 sts).
Next row: P7, turn, sl 1, K back.
　　　　　P6, turn, sl 1, K back.
　　　　　P5, turn, sl 1, K back.
Next and every foll. alt row for now: P.
Next K row: (K9, m1) twice, K2, K2 tog twice, K2, (m1, K9) twice (46 sts).
Next K row: K9, m1, K11, m1, K1, K2 tog twice, K1, m1, K11, m1, K9 (48 sts).

Next K row: K9, m1, K13, m1, K4, m1, K13, m1, K to end (52 sts).
Next K row: K9, m1, K15, m1, K4, m1, K15, m1, K9 (56 sts).
St st 3 rows.
Next K row: K28, m1, K28.
Next K row: K28, m1, K1, m1, K28 (59 sts).

To shape knees

Next K row: K16, K2 tog twice, K19, K2 tog twice, K to end.
Next K row: K14, cast off next 7 sts, K until there are 14 sts on right needle for centre section, cast off next 7 sts, K to end (41 sts).
Next row: P to end, pulling sts tog tightly at cast off sections to shape knees (gaps will be sewn closed later).
Continue straight in st st for 20 rows, ending on a P row.
Next row: K5, (K2 tog, K4) to end (35 sts).

Joining on arms

Next row: P7, cast off next 7 sts, P7, cast off next 7 sts, P7.
Next row: K7, K across sts of left arm, K7, K across sts of right arm, K7 (41).
St st 7 rows, ending on a P row.
Next row: K10, K2 tog twice, K until 14 sts remain, K2 tog twice, K to end (37).
Next row: P.
Next row: K1, K2 tog to end (19 sts).
Cast off.

Head

Left side

Cast on 7 sts and starting with a K row, st st 2 rows.
Next row: K3, K2 tog, K2.
St st 2 rows.
Next row: Cast on 8 sts at beg of row, P11, m1, P to end (15 sts).
Next row: K to last 2 sts, K2 tog.
Next row: P2 tog, P to end.
Rep last 2 rows until 9 sts remain.
St st 2 rows.
Continue to dec at nose end in next 2 rows (7 sts).
Cast off, knitting 2 sts tog at each end of row at same time.

Right Side

Work as for left side, starting with a P row and reversing shaping by reading K for P and P for K.

Head Gusset

Cast on 6 sts and st st 24 rows.
Dec 1 st at each end of next and following 4th row. P 1 row.
K2 tog and finish off.

Tail

Cast on 4 sts and P 1 row.
Next row: Inc 1, K1, inc 1, K1.
St st 7 rows.
Continue to inc at each end of every 8th row until there are 16 sts.
St st 3 rows. Cast off.

Allow the tail to roll in naturally and then tighten the roll a bit more. Slip st the under seam up to top. (About half way along, anchor thread with an extra st, continue sewing up for about 2cm, pull yarn gently to curve tail, anchor with another st and then finish sewing up).

Making up

Body

With K sides tog, fold feet lengthways and sew seam up to markers. Join back seam to about halfway up the back, matching bottom markers. To finish sewing the bottom, flatten out the body so that the lower back seam is at the centre and sew up the horizontal seam that has formed between the feet (see diagram). Fold cast off edges of knees in half and oversew closed, deep enough to prevent the cast off stitches showing on the right side. Turn the right way out.

Fold the arms right sides tog and sew seams up to markers. Turn right way out and from inside of body, sew cast off edge of arms to cast off edge of body.

You really need some artery forceps to turn the limbs out as they are a bit fiddly. Stuff the body but push only the tiniest bit of stuffing into the toe part of the feet but not the 'ankles'. Push plenty of stuffing into the bottom, shaping with your hands at the same time.

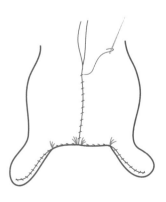

Ladderstitch the rest of the body closed and then stuff the rest of the back. The shoulders need to be shaped with plenty of stuffing but only push a tiny bit of stuffing into the tops of the arms. You will see as you work how they will hang as you stuff and shape the shoulders.

Head

With right sides tog for all sewing up, first join chin seam up to tip of nose. Pin and sew in head gusset. Try to sew edges of gusset to inside of cast off sts at top of head so that they do not show. Turn right side out and stuff carefully, pushing the stuffing well down into the nose first and moulding the head into shape. Do not worry at this point that the head is not the correct shape yet. Inserting the eyes will pull it into the correct shape. Sew head to body, adding extra stuffing as you go to keep the neck firm.

To hold arms to body, either sew tip of paws tog with a couple of sts or knot a length of yarn, take it through into the back and come out just below elbow position. Take a couple of sts of the arm, go through the body to the other side and repeat, pull gently, just enough to keep arms close to the sides and fasten off, sinking the ends into the body out of sight.

Ears

Thread a length of the brown yarn onto a needle, double it up and knot the end. Go into the head through the back of the neck and come out at the side and towards the back of the head. Make 3 sts (about 1cm long) over the top of each other, keeping them loose enough to build up the ear. Take your needle through the head to the second ear position (do not pull thread tightly) and repeat.

Eyes and head shaping

Mark the eye positions with two pins (halfway along the gusset line between nose tip and top of head). With 2 strands of medium brown embroidery thread, darn an eye shape along the seam line around each pin, building up to quite a round shape. It will be easier if you turn the head over to one side to do each eye (see diagrams). If you think the eye 'patches' need to be a bit larger, a brown eyebrow pencil applied around outside of sts is very effective. You could find some photographs of Meerkats to help get them 'just right'.

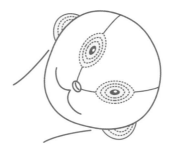

Remove the pins and insert the beads in the same way as for the Duncan bear. Use the 5mm beads for the adults and 4mm for the juniors. Pull the eyes in quite firmly and they will flatten and shape the head. When you are happy with the shape, secure the threads well at the back of the neck then sink them into the body out of sight. With 3 strands of the brown embroidery thread, sew 3 little stitches for the nose and 2 for the mouth as in the photograph.

Sewing tail to body

Sit Meerkat and hold top of tail against bottom in a satisfactory position (seam at underside) so that he can sit comfortably. Pin if necessary or tack with a couple of sts of other coloured yarn. Starting at the top, oversew tail to body about ¾ of the way around, for adult, add a very small amount of stuffing inside top cm and then finish sewing on.

Juniors

Left arm

Cast on 2 sts.

First row: Inc knitwise in each st (4 sts).
Next row: P.
Next row: Inc 1, K 1, inc 1, K1 (6 sts).
St st 3 rows.
Next row: Inc 1, K 3, inc1, K1 (8 sts).
Next row: P.
Next row: Inc 1, K1, K2 tog twice, inc 1, K1.
Next row: P.
Rep last 2 rows twice.
St st 2 rows.

Arm shaping

Next row: K4, m1, K4.
Next and following alt row: P.
Next K row: K4, m1, K1, m1, K4.
Next K row: K4, m1, K3, m1, K4 (13 sts)**.
Next row: Cast off 5 sts, P to end.
St st 2 rows.
Leave sts on a holder for now.

Right arm

Work as for first arm to **.
Next row: P to last 5 sts, cast off 5.
Rejoin yarn and st st 2 rows.
St st 2 rows.
Leave sts on a holder for now.

Body

Starting at feet cast on 6 sts.

First row: Inc knitwise in each st (12 sts).
Row 2: P.
Row 3: K2 tog, K2, K2 tog twice, K2, K2 tog (8 sts).
Row 4: P.
Row 5: Inc1, K1, K2 tog twice, inc 1, K1.
Row 6: P.
Row 7: Rep row 5.
Row 8: P3, P2 tog, P3.
Row 9: K3, m1, K1, m1, K3 (9 sts).
Row 10: P.
Mark each end of row and leave these sts on a holder for now.

Make a second foot exactly the same, then:
Next row: Cast on 4 sts at beg of row, K until there are 7 sts on right hand needle, m1, K3, m1, K3, turn, cast on 4 sts, turn back and K across first 3 sts of first foot, m1, K3, m1, K to end, turn and cast on 4 sts (34 sts).
Next row: P.
Mark each end of last row. This marking is quite important for matching seams and sewing up later.
Next row: K7, m1, K5, m1, K3, K2 tog twice, K3, m1, K5, m1, K 7 (36 sts).
Next row: P.

To shape bottom

Next row: K6, turn, sl 1, P back.
K5, turn, sl 1, P back.
K4, turn, sl 1, P back.
K3, turn, sl 1, P back.
Next row: K7, m1, K7, m1, K2, K2 tog twice, K2, m1, K7, m1, K 7.
Next row: P6, turn, sl 1, K back.
P5, turn, sl 1, K back.
P4, turn, sl 1, K back.
P3, turn, sl 1, K back.
Next and every foll. alt row for now: P.
Next row: K7, m1, K9, m1, K1, K2 tog twice, K1, m1, K9, m1, K7 (40 sts).
Next K row: K7, m1, K11, m1, K2 tog twice, m1, K11, m1, K7.
Next K row: K20, m1, K1, m1, K21.
Next K row: K20, m1, K3, m1, K21 (46 sts).
St st 3 rows.

To shape knees

Next K row: K10, cast off next 7 sts, K until 17 sts remain on left hand needle, cast off next 7 sts, K to end (32 sts).
Next row: P to end, pulling sts together tightly at each end of cast off sts to form knees (gap to be sewn closed later).
St st 4 rows straight *.

To shape back

Next row: K2 tog, K to last 3 sts, turn, sl 1, P to last 3 sts, turn, sl 1, K to end.
Next row: P2 tog, P to end (30 sts).
Continue straight in st st for 6 rows, ending on a P row.
Next row: K8, K2 tog, K to last 10 sts, K2 tog, K to end (28 sts).

Inserting arms

Next row: P6, cast off next 5 sts, P until there are 6 sts on your right hand needle for chest, cast off next 5 sts, P6 to end. You should now have 3 sets of 6 sts.
Next row: K6, K across sts of left arm, K6, K across sts of right arm, K to end (34 sts).
St st 3 rows.
Next row: K8, K2 tog twice, K until 12 sts remain, K2 tog twice, K to end (30 sts).
Next row: P.
Next row: K2 tog to end (15 sts).
Next row: P.
Cast off.

Tail

Starting at tip cast on 3 sts and st st 6 rows.
Next row: Inc in first and last st (5 sts).
St st 7 rows.
Continue to inc in next and every 4th row until 15 sts.
St st 3 rows.
Cast off.
Sew up tail as for adults.

Head

Starting at neck, cast on 12 sts and starting with a P row, st st 3 rows.

Left side

K6, turn and work on these sts only for now.
First row: Cast on 7 sts at beg of row, P these sts and to end of row (13 sts).
Next row: K to last 2 sts, K2 tog.
Next row: P2 tog, P to end.
Cont to dec like this at nose end until 7 sts remain.
Cast off, knitting 2 sts tog at each end of row at same time.

Right side

With right side facing, rejoin yarn.
First row: K.
Next row: P.
Next row: Cast on 7 sts at beg of row, K these sts and to end of row (13 sts).
Next row: P to last 2 sts, P2 tog.
Next row: K1, K2 tog, K to end.
Cont to dec like this until 7 sts remain.
Cast off (in P) as first side.

Head Gusset

Starting at nose, cast on 2 sts.
First row: Inc 1, K1.
Next row: P.
Next row: Inc 1, K2 (4 sts).
St st 3 rows.
Next row: Inc 1, K to last 2 sts, Inc 1, K1.
Next row: P.
Rep last 2 rows (8 sts).
St st 8 rows straight.
Next row: K1, K2 tog, K to last 3 sts, K2 tog, K1.
St st 7 rows. Cast off.

Sew up and complete junior in the same way as the adults.

Meerkat Accessories

Adult Waistcoat

Worked in g. st throughout.
With 3mm knitting needles cast on 36 sts and K 1 row.
Inc 1 at each end of next and foll. alt row (40 sts).
K 4 rows straight.

Divide for front and back

Next row: K6, cast off next 6 sts, K until there are 16 sts on your needle for back, cast off next 6 sts, K6.

First side

Next row: K.
Next row: K2 tog, K to end.
K 8 rows straight, ending at front edge.
Next row: K1, K2 tog, K to end.
K 5 rows, ending at front edge.
Rep last 6 rows.
Cast off remaining 3 sts.

Back

With right side facing, rejoin yarn to next 16 sts, K2 tog at each end of row.
K 18 rows straight.
Cast off.

Second side

Rejoin yarn at inside, armhole edge and K to end.
Next row: K to last 2 sts, K2 tog.
K 8 rows straight, ending at armhole edge.

Next row: K to last 3 sts, K2 tog, K1.
K 5 rows straight.
Rep last 6 rows. Cast off.

Sew up shoulder seams.

If required, with contrast yarn, blanket st all around outer edges.

Scarf

With yellow yarn cast on 4 sts. G. st 8 rows each of yellow, green, blue and light brown (3 times each). Cast off and fringe as for Jim's scarf.

Junior Waistcoat

Worked in garter st throughout.
With 3mm needles, cast on 34 sts.
Inc 1 st at each end of next and foll. alt row (38 sts).
K straight for 7 rows.

To shape right side

Next row: K9, turn and work on these sts only for now.
Next row: Cast off 3 sts, K to end.
Next row: K.
Next row: Dec 1 st at beg of row.
K 2 rows.

To shape front

Next row: K1, K2 tog, K to end.
K 3 rows.
Next row: K1, K2 tog, K1.
K 6 rows.
Cast off.

To shape back

Rejoin yarn at inside (armhole) edge.
Next row: Cast off 3 sts, K until there are 17 sts on right hand needle, turn and work on these sts only for now.

To shape armhole

Next row: Cast off 3 sts at beg of row, K to end.
Next row: Dec 1 st at each end of row (12 sts).
Work straight for 10 rows.
Cast off.

To shape left side

Starting at armhole edge, rejoin yarn to remaining 9 sts.
Next row: Cast off 3 sts, K to end.
Next row: K.
Next row: Dec 1 st at beg of row.
K 2 rows.
Complete as for right side from 'To shape front'.

Make up as for adult waistcoat, adding buttons or beads if required.

Junior backpack

With 3mm needles and DK yarn, work as for miniature dolls backpack. Use size 2¾mm needles for the straps. Each strap to measure 9cm long, unstretched.

Naughty Little Rats

To knit one of these naughty little rats, follow the instructions for the junior Meerkat, making the changes shown below.

Height
Approximately 20cm (7¾in)

Materials
- 1 × 25g or 50g ball of DK yarn in White/Dark Grey.
- Oddments of DK yarn in pink, plus oddments of yellow or blue for jumper.
- 1 pair each of 3mm and 3¼mm knitting needles.
- 1 pair 4mm beads for eyes.
- extra strong thread for whiskers.

Arms

With 3mm needles and pink yarn, work as for junior Meerkat until there are 6 sts, ending on a P row.
St st 2 rows.
Change to 3¼mm needles and blue/yellow yarn.
Next row: Inc 1, K3, inc1, K1 (8 sts).
Next row: K.
Next row: Inc1, K1, K2 tog twice, inc1, K1.
Next row: P.
Rep last 2 rows once.
Complete arms as for Meerkat from 'Arm shaping'.

Body

Starting at feet use 3mm needles and pink yarn, and work as for junior Meerkat, missing out rows 6 and 7.
Change to white/grey yarn on row 9.

Continue as for Meerkat until start of 'To shape back'.
Leave on a spare needle for now.

Jumper

With 3mm needles and blue/yellow yarn, cast on 36 sts and rib 3 rows.
Next row: Rib 5, (K2 tog, rib 6) 3 times, K2 tog, rib 5 (32 sts).
Next row: Hold the spare needle with body sts adjacent to and behind the needle with the rib sts on.
With a 3¼mm needle, K 1 st from each needle together to end. P1 row.
You should still have 32 sts.
With 3¼mm needles, complete as for Meerkat body from * until last but one row.
Next row: K2, (K2 tog) to last 2 sts, K2.
Next row: P.
Cast off.

Head

With 3mm needles and white/grey yarn, cast on 12 sts and P 1 row.
Next row: K6, turn, cast on 8 sts, P these sts and to end of row (14 sts).
Next row: K to last 2 sts, K2 tog.
Next row: P2 tog, P to end.
Continue to dec 1 st at nose end in every row until 7 sts remain.
P 1 row and cast off.
With K side facing, rejoin yarn, cast on 8 sts and K to end.
Dec 1 st at nose end in every row as for first side, reversing shaping. K 1 row.
Cast off.

Head gusset
As for junior Meerkat.

Ears

Make 2 in garter st – With 3mm needles and pink, cast on 5 sts and K 2 rows.
Next row: Inc1, K1, K to last 2 sts, inc1, K1.
K 4 rows.
Next row: K1, K2 tog, K to last 3 sts, K2 tog, K1.
Cast off, leaving a longish thread.

Make up the rats as for the Meerkats. Sew back seam of jumper welt separately from body.

Sew ears on upside down (cast off sts to head), well back on the head and the sides curled inwards. Sew 3 or 4 pink sts for nose. When inserting eyes, do not pull tightly as for the Meerkats as you do not want a flattened face. Attach whiskers as for the mice.

For fluff between ears, thread a length of yarn, double it up and knit end. Take needle in through back of neck and come out at top of head. Pull yarn through and trim to about 2cm. Rep a couple of times. Fluff up threads with end of needle.

Collar

With 3mm needles, cast on 26 sts and rib 7 rows. Cast off in rib. Wrap around and sew bottom edge to neck. Sew up seam at back and fold over.

Tail

With 3mm needles and pink yarn, cast on 3 sts and work in st st for 6 rows.
Inc 1 st at each end of next and every 8th row until 11 sts. St st 7 rows. Cast off.

Sew on tail as for Meerkats.

Fred and Alice

These quirky little mice would be perfect as extra gifts peeping out of the top of a Christmas stocking. They are very easy to make but their limbs are a bit fiddly to stuff. A pair of forceps are ideal for this job but if you don't have any, eyebrow tweezers can be used.

Height
Approximately 23cm (9 in) to top of ears.

Materials
- 1 x 50g ball of 4 ply yarn in mousy colour for both mice.
- Oddments of 4 ply yarn in red and cream for skirt and scarf.
- 1 pair of size 2¾mm Knitting needles.
- Tapestry needle.
- Artery forceps/tweezers for turning and stuffing.
- Small amount of polyester stuffing.
- 1 pair 4mm black beads for each mouse or black embroidery thread **Do not use beads for toys intended for small children**
- Strong black thread for whiskers.
- Dark brown embroidery thread for mouth and claws.
- Very small amount of medium brown yarn for nose or a brown felt tip pen.

Fred and Alice Mice

Body – all one piece
Cast on 28 sts.
Row 1: K13, inc in next 2 sts, K13.
Row 2 and every following alt row: P.
Row 3: K14, inc in next 2 sts, K14.
Row 5: K15, inc in next 2 sts, K15.
Row 7: K16, inc in next 2 sts, K16.
Row 9: K17, inc in next 2 sts, K17 (38 sts).
Continue straight in st st for 15 rows.
Next row: K17, K2 tog twice, K17.
Next row: P.
Next row: K16, K2 tog twice, K16.
Next row: P.
Next row: K15, K2 tog twice, K15 (32 sts).
Next row: P.

To shape shoulders
Next row: *K5, K2 tog twice, rep from * twice, K5 (26 sts).
Next row: P.
Next row: K4, K2 tog twice, *K3, K2 tog twice, rep from * once, K4 (20 sts).
Next row: P.
Cast off remaining 20 sts.
Place a marker at each end of row about 1cm (½ in) up from cast on edge. This will be for tail placement later on.

Head

Side A
Cast on 8 sts and starting with a K row, st st 4 rows.
Next row: K to last 2 sts, inc 1, K1.
Next row: Cast on 10 sts at beg. of row, P these sts and to end of row (19 sts).
Next row: K to last 2 sts, K2 tog.
Next row: P2 tog. P to end.
Continue to dec at nose end in every row until 8 sts remain.

Next row: Dec 1 st at each end of row.
Cast off, knitting 2 sts tog at each end of row at same time.

Side B
Cast on 8 sts and starting with a P row, st st 4 rows.
Next row: P to last 2 sts, inc 1, P1.
Next row: Cast on 10 sts at beg of row, K these sts and to end of row (19 sts).
Next row: P to last 2 sts, P2 tog.
Next row: K2 tog, K to end.
Complete to match first side, reversing shaping.

Head Gussett – make 1
Cast on 2 sts, leaving a long thread to identify nose end. Starting with a K row:
Next row: Inc in each st.
Next row: P.
Next row: Inc 1 st at each end of row (6 sts).
Continue straight in st st until work measures 9cm (3½ in) , ending on a P row.
Next row: Dec 1 st at each end of row.
Continue straight until work measures 11cm (4¼ in), ending on a P row.
Cast off.

Ears – make 4 pieces
Starting at top of ear – Cast on 8 sts and starting with a K row, st st 2 rows.
Next row: Inc in first st, K to last 2 sts, inc 1, K1.
St st 4 rows.
Next row: Dec 1 st at each end of row.
Cast off remaining 8 sts, knitting 2 sts tog at each end of row at same time.

Legs – make 2

To shape foot

Cast on 23 sts. Start with a K row.

First row: Inc 1 st at each end of row.
St st 4 rows.

Next row: Dec 1 st at each end of row.
Cast off 6 sts at beg of next 2 rows.
Continue on remaining 11 sts until work
measures 10cm (4 in).
Cast off.

Arms – make 2

To shape paws

Cast on 6 sts.

Row 1: K2, inc in next 2 sts, K2.
Row 2 and every following alt row: P.
Row 3: K3, inc in next 2 sts, K3.
Row 5: K4, inc in next 2 sts, K4.
Row 7: K2 tog, K3, inc in next 2 sts, K3,
K2 tog.
Row 9: K2 tog, K to last 2 sts, K 2 tog
(10 sts).
Continue straight in st st until work
measures 8cm (3 in), ending on a purl
row. Mark each end of row.

To shape top

K2 tog at each end of next and following
alt row.
Cast off, purling 2 sts tog at each end of
row at same time.

Tail – all one piece

Starting at tip of tail – Cast on 3 sts,
starting with a K row, inc 1 st at each end
of next and following alt row (7 sts).
St st until work measures 8cm (3 in).
Next row: Inc 1 st at each end of row (9 sts).
Continue in st st until tail measures 14cm
(5½ in).
Cast off.

To make up

Sew in and trim all loose threads. Press all
the pieces except the tail with a warm
iron, especially at the edges where they
tend to curl in. Match all pieces knit
sides together to sew up unless otherwise
stated. Use a small oversew st to sew up
the pieces.

Head

Sew the two side pieces together from
front neck to tip of nose. Starting from the
tip of the nose (identified by the long
thread), pin and then sew first one side
and then the other of the head gusset,
taking care that both sides are even. Turn
right side out. Cut a length of medium
brown yarn, pinch the end of the nose
together, wrap the middle of the yarn
around the end of the nose 3 or 4 times
and tie off tightly (may be a bit fiddly and
involve some swearing). Trim and thread
both ends of the yarn onto your tapestry
needle and make 3 or 4 satin stitches
each way across nose, it doesn't need to
be too neat, these aren't posh mice. Sink
the ends of the yarn into the head out of
sight. Alternatively, tie around nose with
body coloured yarn and carefully colour
the nose lightly with a brown felt tip pen.
Stuff the head carefully, moulding into
shape as you go. Leave bottom edges
open for now.

Mouth

With a length of brown yarn or embroidery
thread, sew an upside down V shape just
under the nose for the mouth.

Ears

With right sides together, match and sew
up the ear pieces around the outer edges,
leaving the bottom edges open. Turn right
side out and sew closed. Sew to the top
of the head, either side of the gusset
seam with a pronounced curve. You
should then have a gap of about 2cm
(¾ in) between the bottom of each ear.

Eyes

You can use either teddy looped back
eyes or small beads. They are both
inserted in the same way. Cut a piece of
strong black thread about 20cm (7¾ in)
long and thread one end through an 'eye'
or bead, then thread both ends onto your
tapestry needle. Push the needle down
into the position of one eye (about halfway
between the ears and the nose and on
the gusset seam) and bring it out of the
bottom of the head. Do the same with the
other eye, then pull each pair of threads
to embed the eyes very slightly into the
head. Tie the two pairs of threads and
knot tightly. Trim the ends and tuck them
into the stuffing out of sight. Use a length
of black embroidery thread to sew the
eyes if giving to a young child.

Whiskers

Cut a length of extra strong thread, about
25cm (10 in) long. Thread onto your
needle and then double it up. Push the
needle down into the first position, to one
side and slightly above the nose. Come
out directly under the nose and pull
through until about 2cm (¾ in) of the
threads are left showing. Push the needle
back in about 1 stitch from where you
came out, and bring it out again on the
other side of the nose. Cut the threads to
match the first side. Carefully pull the
threads apart to separate.

Body

Fold the body piece lengthways and sew
the long seam from markers to top, this
will be the centre back seam. Leave the
top and bottom open for now. Turn right
side out and put to one side.

Legs

With right sides together, fold the legs
lengthways and sew up the seam from
the back of the heel, around the feet and
up to the top of the leg. This will then be
the centre front seam. Using artery
forceps, turn right side out and stuff to
within a centimetre of the top. Slip st
closed. Lay out the body with the front

facing. Sandwich the tops of the legs just inside the bottom of the body, with each leg adjacent to the sides. Pin and then backstitch the whole bottom edge closed, working through all thicknesses. You should now have a small gap at the back to insert the top of the tail.

Arms

With right sides together, fold the arms lengthways and sew the long arm seam from the hand up to the markers. This will be the underarm seam. Turn right side out, stuff carefully and sl st the top closed. Sew the arms to the top of the body immediately below the shoulder shaping, working from the back.

Tail

Allow the tail to curl in naturally lengthways and slip stitch from bottom to top cast off edge. Pinch the top edges together and sl st closed (the tail is not stuffed). Push the cast off end of the tail just through the gap in the body and sew in place, make sure all the bottom seams are now closed.

Stuff the body firmly but without stretching the knitting out of shape. Position the head onto the body and sew all around the neck, adding a bit more stuffing as you go to keep the neck firm.

Claws

With 3 strands of brown embroidery thread, make 3 claws on all four paws as follows: Knot the end of a length of thread. Take the needle and thread into the paw, coming out at the beginning of the first claw and pulling the thread until the knotted end disappears into the paw. Make three "claws" and then pull the needle out further up the limb, push the needle back in exactly the same hole, come back out a bit further away, pull the thread to create some tension, snip off close to the surface and the thread should disappear into the limb.

Mice Accessories

Scarf

With cream yarn, cast on 5 sts and K 1 row. Working entirely in g. st, K2 rows in red yarn and 2 rows in cream yarn alternately until scarf measures approx. 23cm (9 in) ending on a cream row.
Cast off.

Fringe

Cut 8 lengths of red yarn, approx. 10cm (4 in) long. Fold a piece in half and thread both ends together onto your tapestry needle. Push the needle through an edge stitch at one end of the scarf and then through the loop, which is formed as you pull the threads through. Pull tightly to knot. Repeat 3 times evenly along the edge of the scarf and then do the same to the other end. Trim the threads to about 1cm (½ in) long.

Skirt

Skirt trim

*With cream colour yarn, cast on 74 sts. Break yarn, join in red and g. st 2 rows ** Starting with a K row, continue in st st for 4 rows. Cast off and leave on one side for now.

Main skirt

Repeat from * to **
Starting with a K row, st st 4 rows.
Next 3 rows: K.
Next row: P.
Next row: K1, (K2 tog) to last st, K1 (38 sts).
Next 2 rows: K.
Next row: P.
G. st 3 rows and cast off.

Press the first piece of work well. With right side facing, pin top edge of first piece just under bottom edge of the main skirt and with red yarn, sew through both layers with a small running st just above cream edging.
Sew up side seam.

Belt

Cut a piece of red yarn about 130cm (51 in) long. Fold in half and, holding both ends, twist it as tightly as you can and then fold in half again, keeping the cord taut to avoid tangling. Tie a knot at each end and trim neatly. Tie around top of skirt and knot at the front.

Necklace

This decoration, or something similar can be found in most haberdashery or craft shops. Simply cut to size and sew at the back to secure. You could also buy small beads from charity shops or car boot sales and thread them onto a length of thread.

Lucy

I was asked to knit one of the mice in these colours for a friends daughter.
She loved this pretty, 'girly' version.

Work as for Alice and Fred with the following colour changes.

Body, Head and Arms

Work in cream yarn.

Shoes

With dark pink yarn, cast on as usual and inc in first row, st st 4 rows. Change back to cream.

After stuffing, thread tapestry needle with matching pink yarn, double it up and knot end. Sew over foot from one side of shoe to other. Fasten off. Sew a white bead to outside of each shoe.

Skirt colour

Dark pink with light pink edging.

Main Skirt

Make a bit longer thus:

Repeat from * to **
Starting with a K row, st st 4 rows.
Next 3 rows: K
Complete last 8 rows as for original skirt.

Ears

Make 2 of the pieces in light pink for inside of ears.

Finish off with strings of pretty beads in shades of pink and white. Tie dark pink ribbon between ears.

Milly

This cute little dog is very quick and easy to knit. She comes complete with bed, coat, 2 blankets, bone and toys. The thread - jointed legs make her fully poseable and her removable coats can be knitted in pattern or plain.
A great way to use up scraps of yarn left over from other projects.

Height
Approximately 10cm (4 in)

Materials
- 1 × 50 g ball DK in medium blue.
- Oddments of DK yarn in white, red, yellow and camel.
- 1 pair of 4mm black beads for eyes (optional).
- 1 pair of 3mm knitting needles.
- Stuffing.
- Black embroidery thread.
- 2 tiny press fasteners for each coat.
- 2 white beads.
- Small piece of ribbon for collar (optional).

Please note: This toy is not suitable for young children

Note: You can use any DK yarn but keep to the same brand for both the dog and coat to ensure a good fit.

Milly

Body and Head

Side A – make 1
Cast on 8 sts.
First row: Inc in every st (16 sts).
Row 2: P.
Row 3: K2, (inc 1, K1) to last 2 sts, K2 (22 sts).
Row 4: P.
Row 5: Inc 1 st at each end of row (24 sts).
Row 6: P*.
Inc 1 st at end of next and following 4th row (26 sts).
St st 3 rows, ending on a P row.
Dec 1 st at beg of next and foll. alt row (24 sts).
Row 18: P.

To shape head
Row 19: Cast off 14 sts at beg of row, K to end (10 sts).
Row 20: Cast on 4 sts at beg of row, P to end (14 sts).
Row 21: K2 tog, (inc 1, K1) to last 4 sts, K4 (17 sts).
St st 6 rows, ending on a K row.
Row 28: Cast off 6 sts at beg of row, P to end (11 sts).
Row 29: K.
Row 30: (P2 tog, P1) to last 2 sts, P2 tog (7 sts).
Row 31: K.
Cast off purling 2 sts tog at each end of row at same time.

Side B – make 1
Work as for first side to *
Inc 1 st at beg of next and following 4th row (26 sts).

St st 4 rows, ending on a K row.
Dec 1 st at beg of next and foll. alt row (24 sts).
Row 19: K.

To shape head
Row 20: Cast off 14 sts at beg of row, P to end (10 sts).
Row 21: Cast on 4 sts at beg of row, K to end.
Row 22: P.
Row 23: K4, (inc 1, K1) to last 2 sts, K2 tog (17 sts).
St st 5 rows, ending on a P row.
Row 29: Cast off 6 sts at beg of row, K to end.
Row 30: P.
Row 31: (K2 tog, K1) to last 2 sts, K2 tog (7 sts).
Row 32: P.
Cast off, knitting 2 sts tog at each end of row at same time.

Ears
Work in G. st throughout.
Cast on 7 sts and K 2 rows.
Next row: (K1, K2 tog) twice, K1.
Next row: K.
Next row: K2 tog at each end of row (3 sts).
Next row: K1, K2 tog.
K2 tog and finish off.

Front Legs – make 2
Cast on 4 sts.
Inc in every st in first and following alt row (16 sts).
Row 4: P.
Row 5: K6, K2 tog twice, K6.
Row 6: P5, P2 tog twice, P5.
Row 7: K4, K2 tog twice, K4*.

St st 7 rows.
Row 15: (Inc 1, K2, inc 1, K1) twice (14 sts).
St st 3 rows.
Row 19: (K2 tog, K4) twice, K2 tog.
Cast off, purling 2 sts tog at each end of row at same time.

Back Legs

Work as for front legs to *.
St st 5 rows, ending on a P row.
Row 13: Inc in first st, K3, inc in next 2 sts, K2, inc 1, K1 (14 sts).
Row 14: P.
Row 15: K6, inc in next 2 sts, K6.
St st 3 rows.
Row 19: K6, K2 tog twice, K6.
Row 20: P2 tog, P3, P2 tog twice, P3, P2 tog (10 sts).
Cast off, knitting 2sts tog at each end of row at same time.

Tail

Cast on 8 sts and st st 2 rows.
Dec 1 st at each end of next and 2 foll. alt rows (2 sts).
P2 tog and finish off.

To make up

With P sides tog, join the 2 sides and sew up all around edges using an oversew st, leaving a gap in tummy. Fold each limb lengthways and sew up, leaving a small gap at back. Turn out all pieces and stuff firmly, carefully shaping as you go (you will find a pair of tweezers or forceps very useful for stuffing the limbs). Close gaps with tiny oversew sts. Fold tail and sew along side, turn out, add a little stuffing and sew in place. Neaten ears and sew on as in photograph (facing forward with a tight curve). Embroider eyes by making tiny sts, one at a time over and over on top of each other or you could use 4mm beads for eyes if the toy is not for a young child. Pinch and shape paws and sew on claws. Embroider nose and mouth. If you wish to add a collar, cut a length of ribbon, wrap around the neck and sew at front.

To attach legs

First pin the legs in position on the body, then remove them, placing the pins where the 'joints' are going to be. Thread a needle with a long piece of body coloured yarn, double it up and knot the end. Sew through the body from one front leg 'joint' position to the other, pulling tightly to indent the body and fasten off. Do the same with the back legs.
With another length of yarn, take a few sts from the inside of the tops of the legs, go through the body to the corresponding leg and do the same. Repeat 2 or 3 times, pulling tightly each time. Keep the sts close together to allow for maximum movement.

Milly's Accessories

Coat

Starting at tail end
With red yarn, cast on 25 sts. Working in g. st for now, inc at each end of first and following alt row (29 sts).

Next row: K2 red, join in white and K1 white, K1 red alternately to last 2 sts, K2 red.

Next row: K2 red, P1 red, P1 white to last 2 sts, K2 red.

Keep the check pattern as set and the first and last 2 sts in red g. st throughout from now on. Make sure you twist the 2 yarns at the beginning of every row to avoid a hole forming.

Rep last 2 rows 3 times.

Next row: K2, K2 tog, pattern to last 4 sts, K2 tog, K2.

Next row: K2, pattern to last 2 sts, K2.

Rep last 2 rows twice (23 sts).

Work 4 rows straight, ending on a wrong side row.

Next row: K2, m1, pattern to last 2 sts, m1, K2.

Next row: K2, pattern to last 2 sts, K2.

Rep last 2 rows once (27 sts).

Right side of neck

Next row: Pattern 8, K2 tog, turn and work on these sts only for now.

Next row: Pattern to last 2 sts, K2.

Next row: Pattern to last 2 sts, K2 tog.

Rep last 2 rows twice (6 sts).

Work 3 rows straight, ending on a P row. Break off white.

G. st 3 rows in red and cast off.

Left side of neck

With right side facing, place the next 7sts on a holder for now. Rejoin red and white yarn, K2 tog, pattern to end.

Next row: K2, pattern to end.

Next row: K2 tog, pattern to end.

Rep last 2 rows twice (6 sts).

Work 3 rows straight ending on a P row.

G. st 3 rows in red and cast off.

Neck border

With right side facing and red, pick up and K 12 sts along right side of neck (starting at last cast off st), 7sts on holder and 12 sts along left side of neck (31 sts).

K1 row. Cast off.

Note – If you think you might find the check pattern too fiddly, just follow the instructions in one colour, the coat will still look very smart.

Belt

Cast on 3 sts and g. st until belt measures approx. 15cm (5.9in) [to fit around tummy and overlap 1cm (½in)]. Cast off.

Sew half of a press fastener to the inside of one end of the belt. Sew the other half to the outside of the other end. Sew centre of belt to centre back of coat. Add a couple of beads. Sew press fastener to neck on corresponding sides.

Bed

Sides – All one piece

Cast on 110 sts and starting with a P row, st st 7 rows.

Cast off 10 sts at beg of next 2 rows (90 sts).

Next row: K1, K2 tog, K to last 3 sts, K2 tog, K1.

Next row: P.

Rep last 2 rows 4 times (80 sts).

Next row: Inc in first and last st.

Next row: P.

Rep last 2 rows 4 times (90 sts).

Cast on 10 sts at beg of next 2 rows (110 sts).

St st 6 rows and cast off.

Press if necessary. With K sides tog, fold side of bed end to end and match up the two pairs of opposite, short end pieces. (see diagram overleaf)

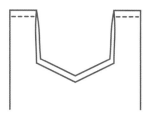

Sew using tiny oversew sts. Keeping K sides together, refold lengthways, match up and sew the shaped front edges, using a small backstitch about 1 st in from the edge to hide cast off edges, (see diagram below).

Turn right side out and press the seams flat with finger and thumb. Pin and oversew the bottom edges together.

Base

Work in g. st throughout.
Cast on 14 sts.

Inc in first and last but one st in next and every following alt row until 28 sts, then every 4th row until 34 sts.
K 6 rows straight.
Dec 1 st at each end of next and every 4th row until 28 sts, then every alt row until 16 sts.
Cast off.
Pin and sew the base to the side piece, using tiny oversew sts on the outside.

Yellow blanket

Cast on 31 sts.
First row: (K1, P1) to last st, K1.
Continue in moss st by repeating the first row until blanket is about square.
Cast off.
Do not press. Blanket st around edges in blue yarn.

Striped blanket

With cream yarn, cast on 30 sts and st st with 2 rows each of cream and camel coloured yard until blanket is about square. Cast off.
Press if necessary and with P side facing, blanket st around edges in blue yarn.

Bone – make 2 pieces

With camel coloured yarn, cast on 4 sts. Starting with a K row:
First row: Inc 1 st knitwise at each end of row (6 sts).
St st 2 rows.
Next row: Dec 1 st at each end of row (4 sts).
St st 12 rows (ending on a P row).
Next row: Inc 1 st at each end of row (6 sts).
St st 2 rows.
Cast off, purling 2 sts tog at each end of row at same time.

To make up

With right sides together, sew all around edges, leaving a small gap along one side to turn and stuff. Turn out and push some stuffing in to the ends of the bone only. Slip st closed.

Ball

With white yarn, cast on 6 sts. Change to blue yarn and inc in every st (12 sts).
P 1 row.
Change to white yarn and st st 2 rows.
With blue yarn, K2 tog across row (6 sts).
P 1 row.
With white yarn, cast off.

With P sides tog, fold lengthways and sew cast on end. Pull up sts tightly and fasten off. Sew sides. Turn out and stuff. Sew up cast off end, again pulling sts tightly before fastening off.

Plaited toy

Cut 12 lengths from your different coloured yarns, each about 18cm (7 in) long. Bunch them together, tie and knot them about 2cm (¾ in) from one end. Divide the longer lengths into 3 and plait for about 4cm (1½ in). Tie and knot again and trim both ends to neaten.

Christmas Reindeer

This pattern is based on the Milly dog instructions, with only small changes for the body and limbs. These pretty little reindeer look nice in a group at the end of the mantelpiece, amongst the festive trimmings.

Height
Approximately 10cm (4in)

Materials
- 1 × 50g ball light brown or fawn 4 ply yarn*.
- 1 pair 2¾mm knitting needles*.
- 3mm beads for eyes.
- Red and black embroidery thread and sewing needle.
- Scraps of red and yellow felt.
- 4 shirt buttons for each reindeer and matching sewing thread.
- 2 pieces of dark brown pipe cleaner or thin jewellery wire wrapped with brown embroidery thread.
- Stuffing.

I have used 4 ply yarn but they can just as easily be made from DK yarn. Use 3mm knitting needles and make the felt coat a little bit bigger to fit, antlers a bit longer and use 4mm beads for eyes

Reindeer

Body for standing Reindeer
Side A
Work as for Milly to start of body cast off row.
Next row: Cast off 14 sts, K to end.
P1 row. Cast off.

Side B
Work as first side to body cast off row.
Next row: Cast off 14 sts, P to end.
K 1 row. Cast off.

Body for sleeping Reindeer
Side A
Work as for Milly side A until *.
Inc 1 st at end of next and foll. alt row (26 sts).
Next row: P.
Dec 1 st at end of next and following 2 alt rows (23 sts).
Next row: P.
Dec at each end of next and foll. alt row (19 sts).
Next row: P.
Cast off.

Side B
As for side A, reversing shaping by increasing and decreasing at beg of rows instead of end.

Head for all Reindeer
Side A
Cast on 10 sts.
P 1 row.
K.1 row.
Cont as for side A of Milly head from the beg of row 20.

Side B
Cast on 10 sts.
K.1 row.
P.1 row.
Continue as for Side B of Milly head from the beg of row 21.

Front legs
As for Milly but work 13 rows straight instead of 7.

Back legs
As for Milly but work 11 rows straight instead of 5.

To make up

Sew up and stuff as for the Milly dog but leave the neck open. Try not to push any stuffing into the toes. Sew up and stuff the head and then sew to body with one reindeer looking ahead, one looking

around to the front and the sleeping Reindeer with his head forward and down. Push a little more stuffing into the neck as you go to make it nice and firm. Attach limbs as for Milly dog, adding shirt buttons if required. Insert eyes as for Milly dog and embroider nose and mouth using 3 strands of black embroidery thread (red for Rudolph).

Ears

Knit as for Milly. Neaten and trim off the cast on thread. Weave the cast off thread down the side of the ear. Fold the ear in half lengthways and sew on to the head as in photo. A pin pushed down the middle into the head will hold the ear in place while you sew it.

Tail

As for Milly.

Attaching antlers

Cut two pieces of pipe cleaner, one 12cm (4¾ in) long and one 8cm (3 in) long. Bend the longest one into a horseshoe shape with a flattened bottom edge. Do the same with the shorter piece and then twist the 2 ends around the longer piece using the diagram and photo as a guide. Oversew to the top of the head between the ears with the reindeer coloured yarn.

Shape and twist the two pieces together

Coat

Cut a piece of red felt 6cm × 3cm (2½ × 1 in) for each reindeer and 1 each of yellow felt 7cm × 3½cm (2¾ × 1¼ in). Place yellow piece and then red piece on reindeer's back. Cut a strip of yellow about 14cm (5½ in) long. Wrap around tummy, overlap a little bit and secure with a nice bead or button.

Sew some pretty gold ribbon around neck and a tiny bell or pretty beads to front.

Nipper and Elliot

My Grandson and I have a lot of fun with these naughty dogs. They like to nibble fingers and if they don't like something they will spit it out!

Materials for small hand puppets

Elliot
- 1 × 25g ball DK yarn in each of black and white.
- 1 × 50g ball DK yarn in White.
- 1 × 50 grm ball DK in blue.
- Oddment of DK in dark pink.

Nipper
- 1 × 50g ball DK yarn in cream.
- 1 × 50g ball DK yarn in red.
- Oddment of DK yarn in medium brown.

Plus, for both puppets
- 1 Pair each size 3¼mm, 4mm and 4½mm knitting needles.
- A piece of 20cm × 24cm (7¾ × 9½ in) lightweight wadding and small amount of stuffing.
- 1 pair 12mm safety eyes for each dog.
- Purchased dog noses or black yarn/embroidery thread.

For adult size hand puppets
- 1 × 50g ball Aran weight yarn in head colours.
- 1 × 100g ball Aran weight yarn in coat colour.
- A pair of 4mm knitting needles (for the collar), 4½mm (for the dog) and 5mm (for coat).
- 1 pair 14mm safety eyes.
- Everything else, including tongue the same as for smaller puppets.

These hand puppets will probably come in for quite a bit of rough play so fairly cheap yarn can be used.

It is quite important to have the forehead stuffed to give the dogs head some shape. It is also very important to place the markers where stated for matching up the pieces when making up.

The instructions are given for the small puppets. If you want to make the larger size just substitute the larger needles and thicker yarn as shown in materials.

Instructions are given for Elliot the Border Collie but they are both knitted up in the same way. Nipper is knitted in cream only with brown ears so the colour changes for Elliot can be ignored.

Head

Right side – make 1
With 4mm needles and black yarn, cast on 30 sts, join in white and cast on a further 6 sts.
Mark each end and the middle st of this row. Stay with each colour given until told to change.
First row: K6 white, 30 black.
Next row: P2 tog, P to last 6 sts, change to white, P4, P2 tog.
Next row: K2 tog, K3, change to black, K to last 2 sts, K2 tog.
Next row: P2 tog, P to last 4 sts, change to white P2, P2 tog.
Next row: K2 tog, K1, change to black K to last 2 sts, K2 tog.
Next row: P2 tog, P to last 2 sts, change to white P2 tog.
Break off white and continue to dec as before until 18 sts remain*.

Shape forehead
Next row: K to last 2 sts, K2 tog. Mark the beg of the row.
Next row: P2 tog, P to end.
Return to decreasing at each end of every row until 8 sts remain.
Cast off.

Left side – make 1
With white yarn, cast on 6 sts, join in black and cast on a further 30 sts.
Mark each end of row.
First row: K30 black, 6 white.
Next row: P2 tog, P4, change to black and P to last 2 sts, P2 tog.
Next row: K2 tog, K to last 5 sts, change to white, K3, K2 tog.
Next row: P2 tog, P2, change to black, P to last 2 sts, P2 tog.
Next row: K2 tog, K to last 3 sts, change to white, K1 K2 tog.
Next row: P2 tog, change to black, P to last 2 sts, P2 tog.
Break off white and continue to dec at each end of every row until 18 sts remain.

To shape forehead
Next row: K2 tog, K to end. Mark the last st.
Next row: P to last 2 sts, P2 tog.
Return to decreasing at each end of every row until 8 sts remain.
Cast off

Head Gusset – Make 1
With 4mm needles and white yarn, starting at back of neck, cast on 18 sts.
Mark each end of row.
Starting with a K row, work in st st for 12 rows.
Next row: K1, K2 tog, K to last 3 sts, K2 tog, K1.
St st 7 rows.
Dec in this way in the next and following 8th row (12 sts).
St st 7 rows.

To shape forehead and nose

Dec as before at each end of next 2 rows (8 sts).
Mark each end of last row for forehead markers.
St st 4 rows, ending on a P row.
Dec as before at each end of next and following 6th row (4 sts).
Next row: P.
Mark each end of row.

To shape mouth

Starting with a K row, inc 1 st at each end of every row until 12 sts.
Work 4 rows straight, change to black and work 2 more rows straight then inc once more as before (14 sts).
St st 13 rows. Mark each end of row.
Next row: K3, K2 tog until last 3 sts, K3 (10 sts).
Cast off in P.

Under side

With 4mm needles and black yarn, cast on 14 sts and starting with a K row, st st 22 rows.
Next row: K1, K2 tog, K to last 3 sts, K2 tog, K1.
Mark each end of last row, this will be where the top and bottom jaw meet.
St st 3 rows.

Cont to dec as before in next and foll. 4th row (8 sts).
Change to white and st st 3 rows.
Dec 1 st at each end of next and foll. alt row (4 sts).
Next row: P.

To shape inside lower jaw

Inc 1 st at each end of next and foll. alt row (8 sts).
Next row: P.
Change to black and st st 2 rows.
Inc 1 st at each end of next and foll. 4th row (12 sts).
St st 3 rows.
Next row: K2 tog at each end of row (10 sts).
Next row: P.
Cast off.

Legs – make 2

With 4mm needles and white yarn, cast on 9 sts.
Inc in every st (18 sts).
Next row: P.
Next row: Inc 1, K to last 2 sts, inc 1, K1 (20 sts).
St st 13 rows straight.
Dec 1 st at each end of next 2 rows (16 sts).
St st 2 rows, ending on a P row.
Inc 1 st at each end of next and every 4th row until 28 sts, and at the same time, change to black yarn when 22 sts reached on one leg. On 2nd leg change to black yarn once 26 sts reached as shown on large puppet or leave 2nd leg white throughout.
St st 3 rows.
K2 tog at each end of every row until 2 sts.
K2 tog and fasten off.

With right sides tog, Fold legs lengthways and sew up. Turn right way out. Stuff lightly, even lighter towards the top. Sew top closed. With seam lying at centre back, use some brown thread to make claws at edges of paws.

Ears – make 4 pieces

With 3¼mm needles and black yarn, cast on 12 sts and starting with a K row, st st 10 rows.
Next row: K1, K2 tog, K to last 3 sts, K2 tog, K1.
Next row: P.
Dec in this way at each end of next and every following alt row until 4 sts remain, ending on a P row.
Next row: K2 tog twice.
P2 tog and fasten off.

With right sides facing, oversew two ear pieces tog and turn right side out. Do not stuff. Sew the bottom edges closed.

Tongue

Knitted in g. st – With dark pink/red yarn and 4mm needles, cast on 9 sts and K 4 rows.
Next row: K3, K2 tog, K4.
K 9 rows straight.
Next row: K2, K2 tog twice, K2.
Next row: K.
Next row: K1, K2 tog twice, K1.
Next row: K.
Next row: K2 tog twice.
Next row: K2 tog and fasten off.

Coat

The coat has a simple 6 row pattern and barely any shaping so shouldn't take long to make. You can of course knit it in plain stocking stitch.

Back

With 4½mm needles and blue, cast on 49 sts and work in g. st for 5 rows.
1st pattern row: K.
2nd pattern row: P.
Rep last 2 rows.
5th pattern row: K1, *P1, keeping yarn at front of row, slip one purlwise, rep from * to last st, K1.
6th pattern row: K1, (P1, K1) to end.
The last 6 rows form the pattern. Rep the 6 row pattern 3 more times.

Start of armhole edging

First row: K.
Next row: K5, P to last 5 sts, K5.
Rep last 2 rows.
Next row: K5, *P1, keeping yarn at front of work, slip the next st purlwise, rep from * to last 5 sts, K5.
Next row: K5, P1, (K1, P1) to last 5 sts, K5.
Rep last 6 rows with edging as set until a total of 8 sets of pattern have been completed from the start.
Leave work on a spare needle for now.

Under side

Cast on 19 sts and work in g. st for 5 rows. Follow the 6 row pattern and edging as for the back but work 9 sets of patterns instead of 8. This should give a little bulge to form a chest of sorts when made up.

Collar

Next row: K to end of row, then K across sts of back thus:
K2, (K2 tog, K1) to last 2 sts, K2 (53 sts). Change to size 3¼mm needles and work in single rib for about 6cms (2¼ in).
Cast off loosely in rib.

To make up

To attach wadding

Fold the wadding in half so that there are 2 layers large enough for the head gusset to be laid on. Pin the gusset piece (not the inside mouth part) onto the double layer of wadding, wrong side down. You will have to flatten out your knitting as you go.

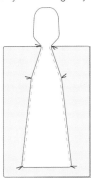

Sew head gusset to wadding

Tack the wadding very closely to the outside side edges of the head gusset with matching yarn or thread, leaving bottom edge open. Cut out so that the wadding is the exact shape of the gusset.

Cut out head gusset and wadding

Turn work over and draw a line across the wadding, between the eye/forehead markers. Backstitch the 2 pieces of wadding together along this line with either yarn or thread but be careful not to sew through into the knitting.

Head

With right sides together, oversew the 2 side pieces to each side of the head gusset, matching markers (see diagram below).

Oversew the underside to the bottom edge of each side piece from the start of the neck to the jaw markers at centre bottom of side pieces and on underside. To form upper mouth, with right sides tog, fold under and sew inside mouth part to bottom of side piece, matching markers and colour changes. For bottom jaw, with right sides tog, fold back inside mouth part and sew to underside, matching markers and colour changes. Turn right side out.

Note - You will see that part of the inside of the upper mouth then becomes the outside when all is sewn in place.

Sandwich and pin the back of the tongue in the opening at the back of the mouth. On the wrong side, oversew in place. Tidy up edges at back of mouth.

To shape the forehead, carefully push some stuffing between the two layers of wadding, up to the line of sewing. It is difficult to say how much really, you will need to stuff and shape and see how it looks. Only stuff a couple of inches or so, you don't need any further back so it should get lighter and then peter out.

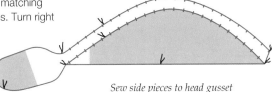

Sew side pieces to head gusset

Ears

Sew the ears towards the back of the head, at an angle facing forward and slightly sideways (see diagram), bringing the outer bottom edges curled in slightly. Fold forward and catch down with a few sts.

Sewing ears to head

Nose

Fix in place as in photograph if using safety nose or darn a nose with some of the black yarn or some embroidery thread.

Eyes

These are placed about halfway between the nose and the ears, about where the markers are and just at the outside edge of the gusset seam.

Coat

Lay out the coat so that the inside is facing. Position and pin the top of the legs into the armholes as shown on the diagram and oversew them to the inside edge of the armhole edging.

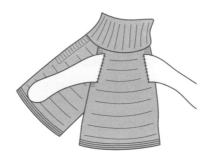

Sewing arms to inside of armholes

The coat is sewn to the head on the right side around the base of the collar. Start by pinning the centre back of the collar base to the centre back, bottom edge of the head gusset then pin the rest on to fit. The underside neck of the coat is about the same size as the front neck of the dog so try to match these together. Backstitch through all layers and when you get to the collar side edges, either sew them up to make a roll neck or overlap a little bit at the bottom and sew on a nice big button.

With right sides tog, sew up the side seams of front and back up to armholes.

50

Miniature Dolls

These are ideal as little dressing up dolls. Their clothes are very easy to get on and off. They have shaped bottoms so are able to sit comfortably.

Height
Approximately 16cm (6¼ in).

Materials
- Oddments of DK yarn in shades of flesh colour for dolls, hair colours, shoe colours and sock colours.
- Oddments of 4 ply yarn in various colours for rest of clothes.
- Brown or black embroidery thread.
- 1 pair each of size 3mm, 2¾mm and 2¼mm knitting needles.
- Tapestry/wool needle.
- Polyester stuffing.
- 2 beads for dress.
- Press fastener for jumper and skirt.
- Forceps or tweezers for turning and stuffing limbs.

The dolls are worked in a DK yarn. As the clothes are so small they are knitted with 4 ply yarn.

I have not stated any clothes colours in the instructions as you may want to use up your left over yarn from other projects.

Dolls

Work in st st unless otherwise stated.

Body and Head

With 3mm needles and flesh colour, cast on 24 sts.
First row: K6, (inc 1, K3) 3 times, K6 (27 sts).
Next row: P.

Shape bottom as follows:
K2, turn and P back.
K4, turn, sl 1, P back.
K6, turn, sl 1, P back.
K8, turn, sl 1, P back.
Next row: K to end.
P2, turn and K back.
P4, turn, sl 1, K back.
P6, turn, sl 1, K back.
P8, turn, sl 1, K back.
Next row: P to end.
Dec 1 st at each end of next and foll. alt row. (23 sts).
*St st 9 rows, ending on a P row.

To shape shoulders and head
Next row: K4, K2 tog twice, K7, K2 tog twice, K4.
Next row: P.
Next row: K4, K2 tog, K7, K2 tog, K 4 ** (17 sts).
St st 3 rows.
Next row: K4, inc in next 8 sts, K5 (25 sts).
St st 10 rows, ending on a K row.
Next row: P2 tog to last st, P1.
Next row: K2 tog to last st, K1 (7 sts).
Break yarn, leaving a long enough thread to sew up back seam of head and body, thread through remaining sts. Draw up tightly and fasten off.

Legs – make 2

To shape shoes
With a chosen shoe colour in DK and 3mm needles, cast on 18 sts.
Starting with a P row, st st 3 rows.
4th row: K3, K3 tog 4 times, K3 (10 sts).
Change to sock colour
5th row: P tightly*.
6th row: K3, K2 tog twice, K3.
St st 2 rows, ending on a K row.
9th row: K.
Change to flesh colour and starting with a K row st st 6 rows.
Next row: Inc 1, K7 (9 sts).
St st 7 rows straight and cast off.

Striped Tights
With chosen colours, knit shoes as before up to end of row 4. Change to white and P tightly. Work the 6th row. Change to pink and st st 2 rows, ending on a K row. Change to white and P row 9 instead of knitting it. Cont in 2 row stripes for 6 rows, then the inc row and remaining 7 rows.

Arms – make 2 pieces

Starting with hands
With flesh colour and 3mm needles, cast on 6 sts. Starting with a K row.
First row: K1, inc in next 4 sts, K1 (10 sts)
Next row: P.
Next row: K3, K2 tog twice, K3.
Next row: P3, P2 tog, P3 (7 sts)*.
St st 10 rows, ending on a P row.

To shape top
K2 tog at each end of next and foll. alt row.
Next row: Cast off, slipping the first st and leaving enough thread to sew to body.

To make up

Head and Body

With right sides tog, sew up centre back seam from cast on edge to top of head, leaving a gap at back for stuffing. Leave bottom edge open for now. Turn right way out and stuff head and shoulders quite firmly. Tie a length of flesh coloured yarn around neck, just under the inc row, pull up tightly and fasten off. With your tapestry needle, tease out the chin and cheek areas to make them nice and chubby. Leave rest of body unstuffed for now.

Legs

With right sides tog, fold legs lengthways and with matching yarn sew up back seam from under foot to about ¾ way up leg using matching yarn. Turn right side out. Stuff shoes with some shoe colour yarn, cut into 2 or 3cm (1 in) pieces. Tease them into a nice shape with your wool needle. Finish sewing back leg seam (on right side) to top and then stuff legs to within 1cm (½ in) of the top. With seam at centre back, sandwich and pin the top of the legs between the lower edges of the body, adjacent to the sides and with a small gap in between. Backstitch through all layers. Finish stuffing body and close gap in back seam.

Arms – make 2

With right sides tog, fold lengthways and sew up underarm seams to start of arm shaping. Turn out and stuff lightly to within 1cm (½ in) of the top. Oversew shaped edges closed at top of arms and then sew to sides of body just below shoulders.

Oversew arms to body with tiny sts, working from the back

Curly Hair

With chosen hair colour and 3mm needles, cast on 24 sts and K 1 row.

To make curls
(which are formed at the back of the next row)
First row (WS): K1, *insert right needle knitways into next st, place your left forefinger behind left needle then wind yarn anticlockwise round the needle and your finger twice, draw through the 2 loops, (keeping the curl on your finger at the back of your work) but before slipping the st off of the left needle, twist your right needle over and K into the back of it. Release curl. Rep from * to the last st, K1.
Next row (RS): K1, (K3 tog) to last st, K1 (24 sts).
Rep last 2 rows twice.

Note: The procedure is a bit tricky to start with but becomes much easier after the first couple of rows. Try to keep your work fairly loose.

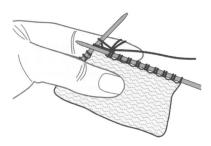

Wrong side facing
Draw through the two loops, keeping the curl on your finger.

Next row: K2 tog across row.
Break yarn a good length from your work, thread through remaining sts using your tapestry needle, pull up tightly and fasten off securely. Fold wig right sides tog and sew up row ends from back to front cast on edge to form a little cap. Turn out and fit onto doll, carefully stretching into place around the back of the head.

With another length of yarn sew around edges and a few sts here and there through the scalp.

You can either leave the wig as it is for nice big curls or trim it close to the head for a short boy hairstyle.

Straight Hair

Cut about 35 × 22cm (8½ in) lengths of yarn. Working with 4 or 5 pieces at a time, back st the centre of the yarn lengths to the seam line at the back of the head, starting 1cm (½ in) up from the neck and finishing just above forehead. To make a fringe, bring forward some of the hair and trim to about 1cm (½ in). Sew some more strands over the top of fringe to stop it sticking up.

Gather each side of hair, tie into bunches and secure to head with 2 or 3 sts midway between top and bottom of head. Trim neatly and tie on ribbon. For plaits, use 3 × 4 strands, any more will be too bulky.

Eyes

Use pins (black headed if you have them) to mark where the eyes are going to be. Cut a length of embroidery thread, brown for the light skin tone and black for the darker shade. Use 2 strands. Take thread through the back of the neck and out at the first first eye position. Make 1 tiny st, about ½ size of a knit st and then oversew this st several times. Do not try to spread out, the eyes will build up to the required size, (with eyes, less is better than more). Take thread through to second eye position and repeat. If you want eyelashes, make 2 tiny sts with 1 strand of thread.

Mouth and nose

The mouth is just 2 sts using 1 strand of embroidery or sewing thread. The nose is 2 tiny sts with 1 strand of light brown (or a couple of dots with a brown felt tip pen if you have one)

Clothes

Dress

With 4 ply yarn and 3mm needles, cast on 60 sts.
G. st 2 rows.
Next row: Join in contrast colour and K 1 st each alternately of the two colours.
Next row: P back, alternating the colours again. Break off contrast colour.
Beg with a K row, st st 12 rows.
Next row: K2 tog to end (30 sts) *.
Next row: K.
Beg with a K row, st st 4 rows.
Divide for front and back.

Front

Next row: K2 tog, K11, K2 tog, turn and work on these sts only for now.
Next row: K2, P to last 2 sts, K2.
Next row: K2, K2 tog, K to last 4 sts, K2 tog, K2.
Keeping first and last 2 sts K in every row, st st 4 rows straight, ending on a K row **.
G. st 2 rows. Cast off.

Back

With right side facing, rejoin yarn to remaining sts.
Next row: K2 tog, K to last 2 sts, K2 tog.
Next row: K2, P to last 2 sts, K2
Next row: K2, K2 tog, K to last 4 sts, K2 tog, K2.
Keeping first and last 2 sts K in every row, st st 6 rows, ending on a K row.
G. st 2 rows.
Next row: K3, cast off next 5 sts, K to end. You should now have 2 sets of 3 sts on your needle for the shoulder straps.
G. st 12 rows on the first set of sts. Cast off. Rejoin yarn and repeat with the second strap.

Sew up side seam of dress to **.
Fit dress onto doll, bring shoulder straps forward and sew to front of dress as in photograph. Sew 2 beads in place.
Note: If you want to be able to remove the dress, sew press fasteners to straps and dress.

Cardigan

Back and Front to armholes
With 2¼mm needles and 4 ply yarn, cast on 45 sts and work in rib for 2 rows.
Change to 2¾mm needles.
Next row: K.
Next row: K2, P to last 2 sts, K2.
Repeat last 2 rows twice.

Right front
K10, K2 tog, turn and work on these sts only for now.
Row 1: P to last 2 sts, K2.
Row 2: K to last 2 sts, K2 tog.
Rep last 2 rows until 8 sts remain.
Next row: P to last 2 sts, K2.
Next row: K2, K2 tog, K2, K2 tog.
Next row: P to last 2 sts, turn.
Next row: K2 tog twice.
Next row: P2 tog and finish off.
Leave remaining 2 border sts on a safety pin for now. Break yarn.

Back
With right sides facing, rejoin yarn.
Next row: K2 tog, K17, K2 tog, turn.
Next row: P.
Dec 1 st at each end of next and foll. alt rows until 9 sts.
Next row: P to end of row, break yarn and leave sts on a holder.

Left front
With right side facing, and rejoining yarn to remaining sts.
Next row: K2 tog, K to end
Next row: K2, P to end.
Repeat the last 2 rows until 8 sts remain, ending on a P row.
Next row: K2 tog, K2, K2 tog, K2.
Next row: K2, place these sts on a safety pin, P to end.
Next row: K2 tog twice.
Next row: P2 tog and finish off.

Sleeves – make 2
With 2¼mm needles, cast on 16 sts and work 2 rows in rib.
Change to 2¾mm needles.
Beg with a K row, st st 2 rows.

Next row: Inc 1, K to last 2 sts, inc 1, K1 (18 sts).
St st 5 rows. Mark each end of row *.
K2 tog at each end of next and every foll. alt row until 6 sts.
Next row: P to end of row, break yarn and leave sts on a holder.

To make up

Sew up sleeve underarm seams to markers. With right sides together, match up and sew raglan seams.
With right sides facing and 2¼mm needles, K the 2 sts on holder at right front, pick up and K 4 sts along right front then K across right sleeve, then the back and then the left sleeve, pick up and K 4 sts along left front, K 2 sts from holder ** (33 sts).
Rib 1 row. Cast off in rib.

Sew on beads or tiny buttons and corresponding press fasteners if you want the cardigan to fasten.

Jacket

Using 2¾mm needles for the rib and 3mm needles for the main parts, work as for cardigan to **.
Change to 2¾mm needles.
Next row: (Rib 7, K2 tog) 3 times, rib 6 (30 sts).
Next row: Rib to end.

Hood

Next row: Change to 3mm needles. Starting with a K row and keeping the first and last 2 sts K in every row, st st 15 rows.
Next row: K13, K2 tog twice, K13.
Next row: K2, P to last 2 sts, K2.
Next row: K12, K2 tog twice, K12.
Continue decreasing 2 sts in the middle of every K row until there are 20 sts remaining, ending on a P row.
To cast off, K10, fold back the hood with right sides tog and your needles horizontal to each other. Cast off 1 st from each needle at the same time using a spare needle.

Jumper

Front

With 2¼mm needles and 4 ply yarn, cast on 20 sts and work in rib for 2 rows. Change to 2¾mm needles and starting with a K row, st st 6 rows *.
Mark each end of last row.

To shape raglan sleeves

K2 tog at each end of next and every foll. alt row until 10 sts remain, ending on a P row.
Next row: K2 tog, K1, K2 tog, turn and P back.
Break yarn and leave these 3 sts on a holder for now.
With right side facing, rejoin yarn to remaining sts, K2 tog, K1, K2 tog.

Next row: P.
Leave remaining sts on a holder.

Back

Work as for front to *.

Back opening

Next row: K2 tog, K8, turn and work on these sts only for now.
Next row: K2, P to end.
Next row: K2 tog, K to end.
Next row: K2, P to end.
Repeat last 2 rows 4 times (4 sts).
Break yarn and leave st on a holder.
With right side facing, rejoin yarn.
Next row: Cast on 2 sts at beg of row, K to last 2 sts, K2 tog.
Mark end of last row.
Next row: P to last 2 sts, K2.
Next row: K to last 2 sts, K2 tog.
Next row: P to last 2 sts, K2.
Rep last 2 rows 4 times (6 sts).
Leave sts on a holder.

Sleeves

Make as for cardigan sleeves, leaving sts on a holder for now.

To make up

Join sleeve underarm seams up to markers. Sew up all raglan seams.

Neck

With 2¼mm needles and right side facing, starting at left back, K across 6 sts of left back, 6 sts of left sleeve, 3 sts of left front, pick up and K 4 sts around front neck, 3 sts of right front, K 6 sts of right sleeve and then 4 sts of right back (32 sts). Work 2 rows in single rib. Cast off in rib. Neaten bottom of back opening with 2 or 3 sts. Sew a press fastener to opening.

Note: You may have to put jumper onto doll feet first, especially one with curly hair.

Shorts

Right side

With 2¼mm needles, cast on 18 sts and rib 2 rows *.
Change to 2¾mm needles.

To shape back

Next row: K3, turn and P back.
Next row: K6, turn and P back.
Next row: K9, turn and P back.
Next row: K across all sts.
Continue in st st for 9 rows, ending on a P row. Mark each end of row.
Next row: Inc 1 st at each end of next and foll. alt row (22 sts).
Next row: P **.
G. st 3 rows. Cast off.

Left side

Work as for right side to *.

To shape back

Next row: P3, turn and K back.
Next row: P6, turn and K back.
Next row: P9, turn and K back.
Next row: P across all sts.
St st 8 rows. Mark each end of row and then complete as for right side.

Trousers

Work as for shorts up to **.
St st 13 more rows, ending on a K row.
K 1 row. Cast off.

To make up trousers and shorts

With right sides together, fold each leg in half lengthways and sew up inside leg seam (widest part is the legs). Turn one leg right way out and fit this one inside the other. Sew up crutch seam and turn right side out.

Skirt

Work as for skirt of dress from beginning to * ignoring the 2 contrast rows and just working the 12 rows of st st (30 sts).
G. st 3 rows. Cast off.

With right sides tog, join skirt seam about ¾ of the way up to the waistband. Sew a press fastener to the waistband to close.

Knickers – All in one piece

With 2¼mm needles and 4 ply yarn, cast on 18 sts and rib 2 rows.
Change to 2¾mm needles.
Starting with a K row, st st 6 rows.
Next row: K1, K2 tog, K to last 3 sts, K2 tog, K1.
Next row: K1, P2 tog, P to last 3 sts, P2 tog, K1.
Continue decreasing this way until 4 sts remain.
St st 3 rows.
Next row: Inc 1, K to last 2 sts, inc 1, K1.
Next row: Inc 1 knitwise, P to last 2 sts, inc 1, K1.
Continue increasing in this way until 18 sts.
Next row: P.

To shape bottom

K to last 2 sts, turn.
Sl 1, P to last 2 sts, turn.
Sl 1, K to last 4 sts, turn.
Sl 1, P to last 4 sts, turn.
Sl 1, K to end.
St st 5 rows, ending on a P row.
Change to 2¼mm needles.
Work in single rib for 2 rows.
Cast off in rib.
With right sides tog, fold and sew up side seams.

Note: The knickers and trousers are not really meant to be worn at the same time, might be a bit too bulky.

Accessories

Baseball Cap

With 3mm needles, cast on 35 sts and
K 1 row.
Starting with a K row, st st 10 rows.
Next row: (K2 tog, K3) to end.
Next row: (P2, P2 tog) to end.
Next row: (K2 tog, K1) to end.
Next row: P2 tog to end (7 sts).
Next row: K2 tog to last st, K1.
Cut yarn and thread through remaining
sts. Pull and fasten off. Sew up seam to
form hat.

Peak

With 2¼mm needles, hold hat upside
down and pick up 16 sts around front of
cap.
Starting with a K row, dec 1 st at each
end of next and every foll. alt row until
8 sts.
Next row: P.
Next row: Inc 1, K to last 2 sts, inc 1, K1.
Next row: P.
Continue to inc in next and every foll. alt
row until 18 sts.
K 1 row. Cast off.

With right sides tog, fold brim and
oversew each side, turn right way out and
oversew to main cap. Press brim firmly
between finger and thumb and make tiny
stab sts very close to the edge and then
along where peak joins cap. This stitching
will flatten and give extra stiffening to the
peak.

Backpack

With 3mm needles and 4 ply yarn, cast on 14 sts.

Starting with a K row, work in st st until knitting measures 9cm (3½ in), ending on a P row. Mark each end of row.

Flap

First row: K.
2nd row: K2, P to last 2 sts, P2.
3rd row: K2, K2 tog, K to last 4 sts, K2 tog, K2.
4th row: Rep 2nd row.

Rep last 4 rows twice (8 sts).

G. st 2 rows then cast off knitting 2 sts tog at each end of row at same time.

With right sides tog, fold rectangle with cast on edges meeting markers and sew sides. Turn right way out.

Cord

Cut a piece of yarn about 40cm (15¾ in) long and thread onto your wool needle. Holding each end of thread, with needle at centre, twist up tightly and then double up. Knot the end. Sew cord as a small running st all round top edge of backpack under markers, starting and finishing at centre front and leaving a couple of cm length at each end for ties. Knot and trim end of cord.

Straps – make 2

With 2¼mm needles, cast on 3 sts and g. st until strap measures 11cm (4½ in). Cast off.

Sew both ends of each strap to centre top of the back of the bag (see diagram).

Sewing straps to backpack

Pixies, Elves and a Leprechaun

The bodies for these little characters are based on the miniature dolls. For these, the clothes are knitted in DK yarn. The Pixies and Elves are made up in the same way. Their boots and hats are different though and Pixies tended to wear a pretty collar while Elves generally wore waistcoats and Jackets.

Height
Approximately 20cm (7¾ in)

Materials for all
- Oddments of DK yarn in flesh pink, green, gold, yellow, red, black, tan, white, brown and light cream.
- Pair of 3mm knitting needles for both toys and clothes.
- Stuffing.
- Dark brown and red embroidery thread and sewing needle.
- Tapestry/wool needle.
- 3mm gold beads for buttons.
- Tiny beads for boot tips and necklace.
- Tiny gold bells.
- Forceps or tweezers for turning and stuffing.

Additional Materials for Leprechaun
- 1 × 25g ball of DK yarn in green.
- Black embroidery thread.

These toys are not suitable for very young children

Note – Unless otherwise stated, work in st st throughout and start rows with a K row.

Pixies and Elves

The colours stated are for the green, yellow and red Pixie. Refer to the photograph for the other colours.

Body and Head

With green yarn, work as for miniature dolls, but work 11 rows of st st at * instead of 9 and changing to flesh coloured yarn at **.
Complete and add features as for miniature dolls.

Arms

Work as for miniature doll arms to *
Change to yellow yarn and K 2 rows.
Starting with K, continue in st st for 8 rows, ending on a P row.
Complete as for miniature dolls from 'To shape top'.
Sew up arms as for miniature dolls.

Pixie boots and legs

To shape boots
With yellow yarn, cast on 20 sts.
First row: K7, K2 tog 3 times, K7 (17 sts).
Next row: P6, P2 tog 3 times, P5.
Next row: K5, K2 tog twice, K5 (12 sts).
Next row: P4, P2 tog twice, P4 (10 sts).
Next row: K4, K2 tog, K4 (9 sts).
St st 2 rows, ending on a K row.
Next row: K.

Legs

Change to red yarn and beg with a K row, st st 10 rows.
Next row: K4, m1, K5.
St st 9 more rows.
Cast off.

Sew up as for miniature doll legs but stuff only very lightly to within 2cms of top. Sew two beads to instep. For the longer, striped legs of the other Pixie, work in 2 row stripes and add an extra 4 rows.

Elf boots and legs

For boots, cast on 28 sts.
First row: K9, cast off next 10 sts, K to end (18 sts).
Next row: P across row, joining up gap tightly in the middle.
Next row: K6, K2 tog 3 times, K to end.
Next row: P5, P2 tog 3 times, P to end.
Next row: K4, K2 tog twice, K4.
Next row: P4, P2 tog, P4.
K 2 rows.

Legs

With colour of chosen Elf, complete as for Pixie legs.

With right sides tog, fold shoe and oversew sole and heel seam closed. Leave top cast off sts of toes open for now. Sew up back leg seam. Turn right side out and with tiny oversew sts, sew the instep seam closed and carry on sewing up the seam to the top front of the boot, pulling the sts tightly as you go to curl up the toe's. Stuff legs lightly as for the Pixies, and sew on beads.

Make up the dolls and attach the limbs in the same way as for the mini dolls.

Ears for both

Left ear

With pink yarn, cast on 4 sts and K 1 row.
Next row: P2 tog, P2.
Next row: K.
Next row: P2 tog, P1.
K2 tog and finish off, leaving a long enough thread to sew ears to head.

Right ear

Cast on 4 sts and P 1 row.
Next row: K2, K2 tog.
Next row: P.
Next row: K1, K2 tog.
Next row: P2 tog and finish off as for left ear.

Neaten and snip off cast on thread, which is at the top of the ear. With cast off thread (which is at the bottom of the ear) and with K side facing, sew the straight side edge to either side of head as in diagram, working from back of ear.

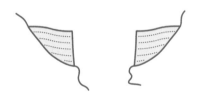

Right and left ears showing cast on threads at top and cast off threads at bottom.

Hair for both

With light brown yarn, sew some tacking sts from centre top of head down to the forehead. With tip of a pin, rough up and split the sts a little bit.

Hat for Pixies

With red yarn, cast on 2 sts.
First row: Inc 1, K1.
Next row: P.
Next row: Inc 1, K1, inc 1 (5 sts).
Next row: P.
Next row: Inc 1, K1, P1, K1, inc 1 (7 sts).
Next row: Cast on 11 sts at beg of row, (K1, P1) on these sts and then to end of row.
Next row: Cast on 11 sts at beg of row, (P1, K1) on these sts then to end of row (29 sts) *.
Next row: K.
Next and every alt row from now on: P.
Next K row: (K4, K2 tog) to last 5 sts, K5.
Next K row: (K3, K2 tog) to end.
Next K row: (K2, K2 tog) to end.
Next K row: (K1, K2 tog) to end.
Next K row: K2 tog to end (5 sts).
Next K row: K2 tog, K1, K2 tog.
Next K row: K2 tog, K1, cast 1 st over the other and finish off.

With tiny oversew sts, sew up back seam of hat on the right side. Attach tiny bell. Fit onto head, with back of hat almost down to the back of neck and sew on through hat rim.

Hat for Elves

Cast on 30 sts and work 1 row in K1, P1 rib.
Starting with a K row, st st 4 rows.
Next row: K6, (K2 tog, K6) to end.
Next and every alt row: P.
Next K row: (K5, K2 tog) to last 6 sts, K6.
Next K row: (K4, K2 tog) to end.
Next K row: (K3, K2 tog) to end.
Next K row: (K2, K2 tog) to end.
Next K row: (K1, K2 tog) to end.
Next K row: (K2 tog) to end.
Next row: K2 tog twice.
Next K row: K2 tog and finish off.

With right sides tog, sew up seam. Turn right way out, carefully teasing the tip of hat out with your sewing needle. Attach tiny bell to the tip of the hat. Sew onto head, bend over the top and catch down with a couple of sts.

A happy little Elf

Collar for Pixies

Work in g. st throughout.
With red yarn, cast on 3 sts and K 1 row.
Row 1: Inc 1, K to end.
Row 2: K to last st, inc 1.
Rep last 2 rows (7 sts).
Row 5: K.
Row 6: K to last 2 sts. K2 tog through back of sts.
Row 7: K2 tog, K to end.
Rep last 2 rows (3 sts).
Row 10: K.
Rep last 10 rows 4 times.

Cast off, leaving a longish thread. With wool needle, weave thread along top straight edge of collar. Place collar around neck and pull up thread and sts to fit. Fasten off and sew up the small back seam. If you have any tiny beads, a little necklace looks nice and adds to the cheerful colours.

Tunic skirt for Pixies

With green yarn, cast on 7 sts and work as for collar, repeating the 10 row pattern 5 times. Ignore the amount of sts in brackets, your maximum amount of sts will go up to 11. Cast off and fit onto Pixie.

Belt for Pixies

With green yarn, cast on 3 sts and g. st about 32 rows or until belt fits quite tightly around top of skirt. Sew belt tog at back seam. With yellow or gold yarn, make 4 sts into a square at centre front of belt for a buckle.

Tunic skirt for Elf

Cast on 33 sts and K 1 row.
Starting with a K row, st st 8 rows.
Next row: (K5, K2 tog) to last 5 sts, K5.
Cast off.

Jacket for Elves

With green yarn, cast on 34 sts and K 2 rows.
Next row: K2, P to last 2 sts, K2.
Keeping first and last 2 sts K in every row, st st 10 more rows.

Right Front
Next row: K7, K2 tog, turn and work on these sts only for now.
Next row: K2, P to last 2 sts, K2.
Continue in st st for 10 rows, keeping border sts correct as before and ending on a P row.
Dec 1 st at end of next and foll. alt row.
Leave sts on a holder for now.

Back
Next row: With K side facing, rejoin yarn, K2 tog, K12, K2 tog, turn and work on these sts only.
Next row: K2, P to last 2 sts, K2.
Keeping border sts correct, st st 10 rows, ending on a P row.
Dec 1 st at each end of next and foll. alt row. Leave sts on a holder for now. Break off yarn and rejoin to last 9 sts.

Left Front
Next row: K2 tog, K to end.
Next row: K2, P to last 2 sts, K2.
Complete as for right side, reversing shoulder shaping.

Collar
With P side of coat facing, K to end of left front, across sts of back and right front (22 sts).
Next row: K2, P to last 2 sts, K2.
Keeping border sts correct, starting with a K row, st st 4 rows. P 1 row. Cast off.
Sew shoulder seams and add some gold beads for buttons.

Belt

Cast on 2 sts and K until belt measures about 10cms unstretched.
Cast off.

Waistcoat for Elves

Worked in garter st throughout.
With colour of choice and 3mm needles, cast on 34 sts.
Inc 1 st at each end of next and foll. alt row (38 sts).
K straight for 6 rows.

To shape right side
Next row: K9, turn and work on these sts only for now.
Next row: K2 tog, K to end.
Next row: K.
Rep last 2 rows twice (6 sts).

To shape front
Next row: K1, K2 tog, K to end.
K 3 rows.
Rep last 4 rows, then K 1 row to end at armhole edge.

To shape shoulder
Dec 1 st at beg of next and foll. alt row (2 sts).
K2 tog and finish off.

To shape back
Rejoin yarn at inside (armhole) edge, K20, turn and work on these sts only for now.
K2 tog at each end of next and 2 foll. alt rows (14 sts).
Work straight for 9 rows.

To shape shoulder

Dec 1 st at each end of next and foll. alt row.
Cast off.

Left side

Rejoin yarn at inside armhole edge,
K2 tog in this and following 2 alt rows
(6 sts).

Complete as for first side.
Join the cast off sts of fronts and back for
shoulder seams.

Leprechaun

Body and head

With green yarn, cast on 27 sts.

To shape bottom
Work as for the miniature dolls bottom shaping up to where it states (23 sts).
Next row: P.
Change to tan coloured yarn.
St st 10 rows, ending on a P row.

Shape shoulders and head
Next row: K4, K2 tog twice, K7, K2 tog twice, K4.
Next row: P.
Next row: K4, K2 tog, K7, K2 tog, K4 (17 sts).
Change to flesh coloured yarn and complete head as for miniature dolls from **.

Ears

As for pixies.

Arms

With pink yarn, cast on 6 sts and work hands as for miniature dolls to * (7 sts).
Change to green yarn and K 1 row.
Next row: Inc 1, K to last st, inc 1, K1.
St st 8 rows.
Mark each end of row.
Dec 1 st at each end of next and following 2 alt rows (2 sts).
Next row: P2 tog and finish off.

Legs

With black yarn, cast on 10 sts.
Inc in each st (20 sts).
Next row: P.
Next row: K4, K2 tog 6 times, K4.
Next row: P.
Next row: K4, K2 tog 3 times, K4.
Next row: P.
Next row: K4, K2 tog twice, K3.
Change to tan/orange yarn.
Next row: P3, P2 tog twice, P2 (7 sts).
St st 5 rows, ending on a K row.

Change to green yarn.
Next row: P.
Next row: Inc in every st (14 sts).
St st 11 rows. Cast off.

To make up

Make up the doll, including features, in the same way as for the miniature dolls.

Hair and Beard

With cream coloured yarn, sew some hair as for the Pixies and Elves. For the beard, cut a long length of cream yarn and double it up. Take the thread in through the back of the neck and come out at the chin. Keeping the thread fairly loose, darn largish sts from the chin down to chest, working first along one side of the face and then the other (see photograph). Fasten off when you are happy with the amount of beard. With a pin, rough up the sts a bit until they look more like hair.

Hat

Knitted in g. st throughout.

Top
With green yarn, cast on 5 sts.
Inc in every st in next and foll. alt row (20 sts).
K 5 rows straight.
Next row: K1, (m1, K4) to last 3 sts, m1, K3 (25 sts).
K 2 rows and cast off. Fold and sew up short edges to form hat.

Rim
With green yarn, cast on 50 sts and K 2 rows.
Next row: K2 tog to end.
Cast off.

Sew rim to hat with the uppermost side curling up slightly (sew the two short ends together and check which side curls upward). If you find you have sewn the rim on the wrong way up, just turn the hat inside out.

Hat band
With black yarn, cast on 32 sts. Cast off. Stretch band and sew around sides of hat, joining short ends.
With gold or yellow yarn, sew 4 sts to make a 'buckle'. Sew hat to head at a jaunty angle, taking the sts deep in and out of head around the inside edge where the rim meets the top.

Belt and Jacket

As for Elves (brown yarn for belt), adding a buckle to belt as for hat.

Bow Tie – optional

Cast on 6 sts and K 4 rows. Cast off. Tie a length of yarn around middle of rectangle, pull up tightly and knot. Tie around neck.

Boots

Sew on buckle as for hat.

Teddies

Jim

Jim is a traditional type bear. He is quite easy to make and is fully poseable with thread-jointed limbs.

Height
Approximately 30cm (12 in).

Materials
- 2 × 50g balls cream DK yarn.
- Oddments of DK yarn in light brown for paws.
- Oddments of DK yarn in red, yellow, dark brown and blue for scarf.
- 1 pair size 3mm Knitting needles
- Brown yarn or embroidery thread for nose, mouth and claws.
- Stuffing.
- 1 pair size 7½mm safety eyes *

*This bear is not suitable for small children unless the eyes are embroidered

Jim

All pieces of Jim are knitted in st st.

Body – All one piece

With 3mm needles, cast on 8 sts and inc knitwise in each st (16sts).
Next and every foll. alt row: P
Next K row: Inc 1, (K2, inc in next 2 sts) to last 3 sts, K2, inc 1 (24 sts).
Next K row: Inc 1, (K4, inc in next 2 sts) to last 5 sts, K4, inc 1.
Next K row: Inc 1, (K6, inc in next 2 sts) to last 7 sts, K6, inc 1 (40 sts).
Next K row: Inc 1, K8, (inc in next 2 sts, K8) 3 times, inc 1.
Next K row: K11, (inc in next 2 sts, K10) twice, inc in next 2 sts, K11 (54 sts).
St st 11 rows**
Dec 1 st at each end of next and foll. alt row (50 sts).
St st 11 rows.
Next row: Inc 1 st at each end of next and foll. alt row (54 sts).
St st 3 rows.

To shape shoulders
Next row: Sl 1, K2 tog, K8, K2 tog twice, K24, K2 tog twice, K8, k2 tog, K1.
St st 3 rows.
Next row: K9, K2 tog twice, K22, K2 tog twice, K9.
Next row: P.
Next row: Sl 1, K2 tog, K5, K2 tog twice, K20, K2 tog twice, K5, K2 tog, K1.
Next row: P6, P2 tog twice, P18, P2 tog twice, P6.
Next row: Sl 1, K2 tog, K2, K2 tog twice, K5, K2 tog, K2, K2 tog, K5, K2 tog twice, K2, K2 tog, K1 (26 sts). Cast off.

Head

First side
Cast on 13 sts.
First row: K.
Next row: Inc 1 st at each end of row (15 sts).
Next row: Inc 1 st at beg of row.
Next row: Inc 1 st at end of row.
Rep last 2 rows twice (21 sts).
St st 4 rows (finishing on a P row).

To shape nose
Next row: Cast off 4 sts at beg of row.
Next row: Dec 1 st at end of row.
Next row: Cast off 4 sts at beg of row, slipping the first st (12 sts).
Next row: Dec 1 st at beg of row.
Next row: K.
Dec 1 st at each end of next 2 rows.
Next row: Cast off remaining 7 sts, purling 2 sts together at each end of row at same time.

Second side
Cast on 13 sts.
First row: P.
Next row: Inc 1 st st at each end of row.
Next row: Inc 1 st at beg of row.
Next row: Inc 1 st at end of row.
Rep last 2 rows twice (21 sts).
St st 4 rows (finishing on a K row).

To shape nose
Next row: Cast off 4 sts at beg of row.
Next row: Dec 1 st at end of row.
Next row: Cast off 4 sts at beg of row, slipping the first st (12 sts).
Next row: Dec 1 st at beg of row.
Next row: P.
Dec 1 st at each end of next 2 rows.
Next row: Cast off remaining 7 sts, knitting 2 sts tog at each end of row at same time.

Head Gusset – make 1

Starting at back neck edge.
Cast on 2 sts. Inc in each st knitwise (4 sts).
Next row: P.
Inc 1 st at each end of next and every foll.
4th row until 14 sts.
St st 9 rows (ending on a P row).

To shape nose

Dec 1 st at each end of next and every alt row until 6 sts.
St st 7 more rows.
K2 tog, K2, K2 tog. Cast off.

Ears – make 4 pieces

Cast on 10 sts. Beginning with a K row, st st 4 rows.
Dec 1 st at each end of next 2 rows.
Cast off remaining 6 sts, knitting 2 sts tog at each end of row at same time and leaving a long thread.

Right Arm – make 1

Beg. at paw, with contrast colour, cast on 4 sts.
Inc 1 st at each end of next and foll. alt row (8 sts).
Next row: P.
Inc 1 st at beg of next and foll. alt row (10 sts).

Next row: P.
Next row: Inc 1 st at beg and dec 1 st at end of row.
Next row: P.
Rep last 2 rows twice.
Next row: Dec 1 st at end of row *.
Break yarn and leave these sts on a holder for now.
With main colour yarn, cast on 4 sts and inc 1 st at each end of next and foll. alt row (8 sts).
Next row: P.
Next row: Inc 1 st at end of row and foll. alt row (10 sts).
Next row: P.
Next row: Dec 1 st at beg and Inc 1 st at end of row.
Next row: P.
Rep last 2 rows twice.
Next row: Dec 1 st at beg of row (9 sts) **.

Joining paw pads to arms

Next row: P to end of row, then across sts on holder.
Next row: K8, K2 tog, K to end (17 sts).
Next row: P.
Inc 1 st at each end of next and every foll. 6th row until 23 sts.
St st 5 rows straight.
Next row: K2 tog, K7, K2 tog twice, K8, K2 tog.
Next row: P.
Next row: K2 tog, K5, K2 tog twice, K6, K2 tog.
Next row: P6, P2 tog, P7.
Cast off remaining 14 sts, knitting 2 sts tog at each end of row at same time.

Left Arm – make 1

With main colour, work as for right arm from beg to *
With contrast colour, work from * to ** break yarn, rejoin main colour and continue from **

Legs – make 2

Cast on 30 sts.
Starting K, st st 4 rows.
Dec 1 st at each end of next and foll. alt row (26 sts).
Next row: P.
Cast off 4 sts at beg of next 2 rows (18 sts).
St st 2 rows.
Inc 1 st at each end of next and every foll. 4th row until 28 sts.
St st 5 rows.
Next row: K2 tog, K10, K2 tog twice, K10, K2 tog.
Next row: P.
Next row: K2 tog, K8, K2 tog twice, K8, K2 tog.
Cast off remaining 20 sts, purling 2 sts tog at each end of row at same time.

Soles – make 2

Cast on 3 sts with contrast yarn.
Inc 1 st at each end of next and every foll. alt row until 9 sts.
St st 9 rows.
Dec 1 st at each end of next and foll. alt row (5 sts).
Cast off, purling 2 sts tog at each end of row at same time.

To make up

Sew all pieces K sides tog.

Body

Fold lengthways, pin and sew up from bottom to top, leaving a gap about halfway for turning and stuffing. The seam lies at the centre back of the bear. Stuff firmly and leave on one side for now.

Head

Pin and sew the two side pieces from front neck to tip of nose. Pin and sew the head gusset to both sides of the head, starting at the nose and working round to the back of the head, adjusting to fit and making sure both sides are even. Stuff temporarily and position eyes (try different positions or refer to the photograph). When you are happy with them, carefully remove them and make a marker st where the shanks are to go. Remove the stuffing and fit the eyes securely.

Stuff carefully, filling out the nose and shaping the head, then sew to the body all around neck edges, pushing in more stuffing before finally closing the seam. Embroider a nose and mouth.

Ears

Match up the pairs of ears, pin and sew up around the curved edges, leaving the bottom edge open. Turn right way out, press flat and oversew closed. Sew quite well back on the head and about halfway across the gusset seams, pulling the bottom corners forward to make a nice curve.

Arms and Legs

Fold each arm lengthways, pin and sew up, leaving a small gap at the back for turning and stuffing. Turn out and stuff carefully, check they match in size and then sew up the gap in the seams.

Fold each leg in half lengthways, pin and sew around the top and down the front, leaving a small gap for stuffing and the bottom edges open. Pin, adjust, and sew the soles to the feet. Turn out and stuff, shaping the feet carefully and then close the seam.

With 3 strands of black or brown embroidery thread, make 3 claws on all four paws.

Attaching arms and legs

Find the best position for the limbs by pushing a knitting needle through limbs and body as if thread jointing. Can he sit comfortably? Remove limbs for now, marking required joint positions. With a long length of yarn, doubled and knotted, sew through from one limb position to another and pull quite tightly to create 'sockets'. Sew inside of limb tops to each side of body securely, matching joint markers, taking the yarn back and forth through the body after each st.

Accessories

Scarf

Worked in g. st.
With red, cast on 90 sts and K in stripes of 2 rows red, 3 rows yellow, 1 row dark brown and 2 rows blue.
Cast off in blue.
Fringe by cutting 10 lengths of yarn about 10cm (4 in) long. Fold a length in half and thread folded end onto tapestry needle. Take needle through end edge of scarf and draw loop through. Remove needle. Pull the two ends through the loop and pull gently to secure. Repeat 4 times and then along other end of scarf. Trim to neaten.

Oscar

Oscar is basically the same bear as Jim, knitted in a thicker yarn. He has a slightly longer body, nose and arms and has contrast features.

Height
Approximately 45cm (17¾ in).

Tension
Not really important but try to use the same thickness yarns for main, contrast and waistcoat colours

Materials
- 1 × 100g ball medium brown aran weight yarn.
- Oddment of oatmeal colour aran weight yarn.
- 1 × 25g ball DK yarn in yellow.
- Oddment of red for waistcoat edging if required.
- Size 4mm knitting needles for bear and waistcoat.
- Stuffing.
- 1 pair size 12mm safety eyes.
- 4 sets 35mm plastic joints.
- Black yarn or embroidery thread for nose, mouth and claws.
- 2 press fasteners.
- 2 small buttons.

Oscar

Note – Always twist the 2 yarns together when changing colour to prevent a gap forming. Stay with each colour until told to change.

Head

First side
With brown yarn, cast on 13 sts.
1st row: Join in contrast yarn and K first st, change to brown yarn and K to end.
2nd row: Inc 1, P to last st, change to contrast yarn and inc 1.
3rd row: Inc 1, K1, change to brown yarn and K to end.
4th row: P to last 3 sts, change to contrast yarn, P1, inc 1, P1.
5th row: Inc 1, K3, change to brown yarn and K to end.
6th row: P to last 5 sts, change to contrast yarn, P3, inc 1, P1.
7th row: Inc 1, K5, change to brown yarn and K to end.
8th row: P to last 7 sts, change to contrast yarn, P5, inc 1, P1.
9th row: Inc 1, K7, change to brown yarn and K to end.
10th row: P to last 9 sts, change to contrast yarn, P7, inc 1, P1 (22 sts).
Keeping colours as set, st st 4 rows and then follow instructions for Jim from nose shaping, casting off 5 sts at the beg of the 2 K rows instead of 4. Break contrast yarn when finished with it.

Second side
Work as for first side reversing colours and shaping by starting with a P row and reading P for K and K for P to the end.

Head gusset
As for Jim until there are 10 sts remaining when decreasing for nose, ending on a P row. Change to contrast colour yarn and complete as for Jim.

Ears – make 4 pieces

Make 2 pieces in brown yarn and 2 in oatmeal coloured yarn.
Cast on 12 sts. Complete as for Jim.

Legs

As for Jim but cast on 32 sts instead of 30 and cast off 5 sts at beg of the 2 rows to shape foot instead of 4.
Inc up to 26 st instead of 28. St st 11 rows for length.
To decrease at top of legs.
Next row: K2 tog, K9, K2 tog twice, K9, K2 tog.
Next row: P.
Next row: K2 tog, K7, K2 tog twice, K7, K2 tog.

Arms

As for Jim, adding 4 extra rows to length before shaping top.

Soles

As for Jim, working 2 extra rows to lengthen slightly.

Body

As for Jim but st st 15 rows twice instead of 11 to lengthen body.

To make up

Make up Oscar as for the Jim bear. You could thread joint the limbs on or use the plastic joints as I have, which I find look nicer on this larger bear. They can be found in most yarn and haberdashery shops and are quite easy to insert. Take care to match the contrast colour on the muzzle pieces when making up the head. The head is sewn to the body as for Jim.

Accessories

Waistcoat

Worked in g. st. There is no right or wrong side so both fronts are the same.

Fronts – make 2

With 4mm needles and yellow yarn, cast on 2 sts.
Inc 1 st at each end of next and every foll. alt row until 20 sts.
Knit straight until work measures 7cm (2¾ in) from the beginning.

To shape armhole

Cast off 2 sts at beg of next and 2 foll. alt rows (14 sts).
K 3 rows, ending at side edge.

To shape front edge

Next row: K to last 3 sts, K2 tog, K1.
K 3 rows.
Continue to dec in next and every 4th row until 8 sts remain, ending at front edge.
Next row: K.

To shape shoulders

Next row: Cast off 2 sts, K to end.
Next row: K.
Next row: Cast off 2 sts, K2 tog, K1.
Next row: K.
Cast off remaining 3 sts.

Back

Cast on 36 sts and work straight until work measures the same as side edges of fronts up to the armhole shaping.

To shape armhole

Cast off 2 sts at beg of next 6 rows (24 sts).
Continue straight until back measures the same as fronts to top of shoulders, finishing on a wrong side row.

Shoulders

Cast off 2 sts at beg of next 6 rows.
Cast off remaining 12 sts.

Pocket

Cast on 6 sts and K 1 row.
Inc at beg and end of next and foll. alt row. (10 sts).
K 6 rows straight. Cast off.

Sew up shoulder and side seams. Blanket st around outside edges with red yarn. Sew press fasteners to front edges of waistcoat and buttons to the outside over the top of the fasteners (there are no button holes). Sew on pocket as in photograph.

Duncan

This miniature bear is very quick to knit but a bit fiddly to make up because of the small pieces. A pair of forceps or tweezers are needed to turn and stuff him. He is ideal as a collector's bear, mascot or pocket sized friend.
He is not suitable for young children because of his size and the tiny bead eyes.

Height
Approximately 13cm (5 in).

Materials
- Oddments of 4 ply yarn in the colour of your choice for bear, jacket and scarf.
- A pair of 2¼mm knitting needles for bear and clothes.
- Size 3mm black beads.
- Black sewing thread and small needle.
- Small amount of polyester stuffing.
- Tapestry/wool needle.
- Black or brown embroidery thread for nose, mouth and claws.
- Forceps or tweezers.
- 3 × tiny press fasteners for jacket.

**This bear is not suitable
for young children**

Duncan

Body and Head – all one piece

Cast on 8 sts
Row 1: Inc in each st (16 sts).
Row 2: P.
Row 3: Inc in each st (32 sts).
St st 7 rows.
Row 11: Dec 1 st at each end of row.
St st 9 rows.
Row 21: Inc at each end of row.
St st 3 rows.
Row 25: K6, K2 tog, K6, K2 tog twice, K6, K2 tog, K6 (28 sts).
Row 26: P.
Row 27: (K2 tog, K4) twice, K2 tog twice, (K4, K2 tog) twice (22 sts).
Row 28: P.
Row 29: K2 tog, K4, K2 tog, K6, K2 tog, K4, K2 tog (18 sts).
Row 30: P2 tog, P5, P2 tog twice, P5, P2 tog (14 sts).
Row 31: K.

To shape head
Row 32: Inc 1, P5, inc in next 2 sts, P5, inc 1.
Row 33: K8, inc in next 2 sts, K8.
Row 34: P9, inc in next 2 sts, P9.
Row 35: K10, inc in next 2 sts, K10.
Row 36: P11, inc in next 2 sts, P11.
Row 37: K12, inc in next 2 sts, K12 (28 sts).
Row 38: P14, turn and work on these sts only for now.

To shape one side of nose
Next row: Cast off 6 sts, K to last 2 sts, K2 tog.
Next row: P.
Next row: K2 tog, K3, K2 tog.
Cast off, slipping the first st

To shape other side of nose
Next row: With P side facing, rejoin yarn, cast off 6 sts, P to last 2 sts, P2 tog.
Next row: K.
Next row: P2 tog, P3, P2 tog.
Cast off, slipping the first st.

Head Gusset
Beg at nose, cast on 2 sts, leaving a long thread.
First row: Inc in each st.
St st 5 rows.
Inc at each end of next and foll. alt row (8 sts).
St st 9 rows.
Dec at each end of next and foll. alt row.
Next row: P.
Next row: K2 tog twice, pass one st over the other and finish off.

Ears – make 2

Worked in G. st.
Cast on 8 st and K 3 rows.
Next row: K2 tog, K4, K2 tog.
Cast off, knitting 2 sts tog at each end of row at same time and leave a long thread.

Arms – make 2

Starting at paw, cast on 3 sts.
Row 1: Inc in each st (6 sts).
Row 2: P.
Row 3: Inc 1, K1, inc in next 2 sts, K1, inc 1 (10 sts).
Row 4: P.
Row 5: Inc 1, K2, K2 tog twice, K2, inc 1 (10 sts).
Row 6: P.
Rep rows 5 and 6 twice.
St st 6 rows.

Row 17: Inc 1, K to last 2 sts, inc 1, K1 (12 sts).
St st 5 rows.
Row 23: K2 tog, K2, K2 tog twice, K2, K2 tog (8 sts).
Row 24: P.
Row 25: (K2 tog, K1) twice, K2 tog.
Cast off, slipping the first st.

Legs – make 2

Cast on 20 sts. Starting with a P row, st st 2 rows.

To shape toes

Row 3: Dec 1 st at each end of row.
Row 4: Cast off 4 sts at beg of row, K to last 4 sts, cast off 4 sts (10 sts) and break yarn.
Row 5: Rejoin yarn and P.
Inc 1 st at each end of row and every foll. 4th row until 16 sts.
St st 5 rows.
Row 20: K2 tog, K4, K2 tog twice, K4, K2 tog.
Row 21: P.
Row 22: K2 tog, K2, K2 tog twice, K2, K2 tog.
Cast off in purl.

Soles

Cast on 3 sts.
Row 1: Inc at each end of row knitwise (5 sts). St st 8 rows.
Row 10: Dec 1 st at each end of row.
Row 11: Cast off, slipping the first st.

To make up

Press all pieces lightly. Darn in and trim all loose ends except the long thread at the top of the ears and at the nose end of the gusset.

Match all pieces purl sides together to sew up. Use an oversew stitch and sew very small stitches quite close together, checking frequently that the seams are still aligned. Use a ladderstitch to close gaps in seams after stuffing.

Head and Body

Sew 1 or 2 sts to neaten off the seam at the tip of the nose.

With purl sides together, sew the head gusset to both sides of the head from the nose to the back of the neck, adjusting to fit. The long thread you left when knitting the gusset will identify which is the nose end. Join the body pieces from the back of the neck to about 1cm (½ in) down the shoulders and back and from the lower back to the bottom. You should now have a gap in the back for turning and stuffing. Turn right side out and stuff carefully, filling out the nose first and moulding into shape as you go. Close the back opening. Tie a piece of the same colour yarn around the neck and pull firmly to define the neck and shoulders. Tie a knot and sink the ends of the thread into the body out of sight.

Ears

Sew in and trim off the shorter cast on thread. Thread the long cast off thread at the top of an ear onto your needle. Weave this thread through the sts at the edge of one side of the ear down to the base, and pull slightly to 'round off' the top of the ear, then take a couple of sts to anchor the thread. Pin and sew the ears to head, almost at the back of the head and over the gusset line.

Eyes

Decide on the position of the eyes and mark with 2 pins. Thread each eye onto a long strand of black thread, double it up and then thread both ends onto your tapestry needle. Push the needle into the eye position and then through to and out at the back of the neck, pulling the thread ends through. Leave them hanging for now and repeat with the other eye, bringing the needle and threads out at the same place at the back of the head. Pull both sets of threads to embed the eyes,

tie off securely, trim and sink the ends into the head out of sight.

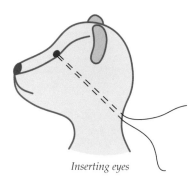

Inserting eyes

Noses and mouth

With 2 strands of embroidery thread, sew a small neat triangle for the nose and 2 or 3 sts for the mouth.

Arms

With purl sides together, fold each arm lengthways and sew up the seams leaving a small gap for turning and stuffing at the back Turn out and stuff carefully, then sew up the gap.

Legs

With P sides tog, sew up back leg seam, leaving bottom edge open and a small gap for turning and stuffing. Sew in the soles. Turn out and stuff then close gap.

Sew 3 tiny claws to all 4 paws.

Attaching the limbs

This little bear is thread-jointed. First pin the arms and legs to the body, the top of the arms a little way down from the top of the body and the top of the legs about 1cm (½ in) up from teddies bottom (check that he can sit correctly). Remove the arms and legs for now, replacing the pins in the exact position where the limb 'joints' are going to be. To attach the legs, thread a tapestry needle with a long piece of body coloured yarn and double it up. Push the needle through one side of the body at the pin position, leaving a long thread, and through one leg, go back into the leg through exactly the same hole you came out of, but come out of the inside of the leg a couple of sts away from where you went in. Go back through the body and into the second leg and then back into the same hole of this leg as before, bringing the needle out between the leg and the body (back to where you started) Pull the threads tightly, knot, then rethread and sink ends into the body out of sight. Attach the arms in exactly the same way.

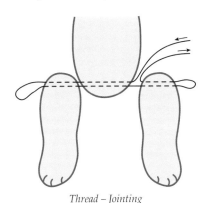

Thread – Jointing

Accessories

Jacket

Back and Fronts – All one piece
Cast on 43 sts.
First row: K2, P1, (K1, P1) to last 2 sts, K2.
Next row: K3, (P1, K1), to last 2 sts, K2.
Next row: K.
Next row: K2, P to last 2 sts, K2.
Repeat last 2 rows twice.

Right Front
Next row: K9, K2 tog, turn and work on these sts only for now.
Next row: P to last 2 sts, K2.
Next row: K to last 2 sts, K2 tog.
Next row: P to last 2 sts, K2.
Rep last 2 rows 4 times (5 sts), break yarn

and leave sts on a holder for now.

Back
With right side facing, rejoin yarn to remaining sts.
Next row: K2 tog, K17, K2 tog, turn and work on these sts only for now.
Next row: P.
Continue to decrease as in last 2 rows until 9 sts remain, ending on a P row. Break yarn and leave sts on a holder.

Left Front
With right side facing rejoin yarn to remaining 11 sts.
Next row: K2 tog, K to end.
Next row: K2, P to end.
Rep last 2 rows 5 times (5 sts). Leave sts on a holder for now.

Sleeves
Cast on 15 st.
First row: K1, (P1, K1) to end.
Next row: P1, (K1, P1) to end.
St st 2 rows.
Inc 1 st at each end of next and foll. alt row (19 sts).
St st 3 rows. Mark each end of row.

To shape top
Dec 1 st at each end of next and every foll. alt row until 7 sts.
Next row: P to end and leave sts on a holder.

To make up
Press all the pieces under a damp cloth. With right sides facing, sew sleeve seams from cuff to markers. Turn out, fit into the jacket and sew up the raglan seams.

With right sides facing, slip the sts from holders onto a knitting needle and K across them in the

following order: 5 sts of right front, 7 sts of right sleeve, 9 sts of back, 7 sts of left sleeve and 5 sts of left front (33 sts).
Next row: K2, (P2, P2 tog), to last 3 sts, P1, K2 (26 sts).

To shape neckline and hood
Next row: Cast off 2 sts, K1, (P1, K1) to last 2 sts, K2.
Next row: Repeat last row (22 sts).
Starting with a K row and keeping the first and last 2 sts K in every row (for hood border), work 12 rows in st st.
Next row: K11, turn and work on these sts only for now *.
Next row: P2 tog, P to last 2 sts, K2.
Next row: K.
Continue to decrease at back edge on next and every alt row until 8 sts remain. Cast off.
With right sides facing rejoin yarn to second side of hood.
Next row: K to end.
Next row: K2, P to last 2 sts, P2 tog.
Repeat the last 2 rows until 8 sts remain. Cast off.
Sew up back hood seam from * to g. st border and rest of jacket seams.
Sew press fasteners to jacket borders.

Harriet

This little bear is very quick and easy to make. Her head is knitted in one piece, as is her body and each limb. She is ideal as a toy for younger children as there are no little pieces to pull off. Even her ears are slotted into her head and sewn from the inside.

Height
Approximately 21cm (8¼ in).

Length of bed
Approximately 30cm (12 in).

Materials for Bear
- 1 × 50g ball DK yarn in sand / fawn colour (this would be enough to make about 3 bears).
- Oddments of DK yarn for clothes in lilac, white, baby denim and soft yellow.
- A pair of 3mm needles for bear.
- A pair of 3¼mm needles for clothes.
- Small amount of stuffing.
- 4mm white beads.

Note
Tension is not really important but try to use the same thickness yarns for the bear and clothes or they might not fit.

Materials for Bed
- 2 × 50g balls DK yarn in cerise.
- 1 × 50g ball DK yarn in pale pink.
- Oddment of white yarn.
- A pair each of 3¼mm and 4mm knitting needles.
- Oddment of light blue felt.
- Stuffing for pillow.
- 3 medium press fasteners.
- A few sequins if required.

Harriet Bear

Right Leg
Starting with feet, cast on 6 sts.
First row: Inc knitwise in every st (12 sts).
Next row: P.
Next row: Repeat first row (24 sts).
St st 3 rows *.
Next row: K3, K2 tog 6 times, K9.
Next row: P.
Next row: K3, K2 tog 3 times, K9.

To shape legs
Continue straight in st st for 9 rows.
Next row: Inc 1, K to last 2 sts, inc 1, K1 (17 sts).
St st 7 rows, ending on a P row
Mark each end of row ** and leave sts on a holder for now.

Left leg
Work as for right leg, reversing shaping from * thus:
Next row: K9, K2 tog 6 times, K3.
Next row: P.
Next row: K9, K2 tog 3 times, K3.
Complete as for left leg from 'To shape legs' to **.

Joining legs to body
Next row: Inc 1, K to last 2 sts, inc 1, K1, join in left leg thus: inc 1, K to last 2 sts, inc 1, K1 (38 sts).
Next row: P.
Next row: Inc 1, K to last 2 sts, inc 1, K1.
Next row: P.
Next row: K10, turn, sl 1, P back.
Next row: K8, turn, sl 1, P back.
Next row: K6, turn, sl 1, P back.
Next row: K4, turn, sl 1, P back.
Next row: K2, turn, sl 1, P back.
Next row: K to end.

Next row: P10, turn, sl 1, K back.
Continue down to 2 sts as with K rows.
Next row: P to end.
St st 14 rows straight *.

To shape left back
Next row: K8, K2 tog, turn and work on these sts only for now.
Next row: P.
Next row: K to last 2 sts, K2 tog.
Continue to dec in this way at armhole edge until 5 sts remain, ending on a P row. Cast off.

Front
With K side facing, rejoin yarn, K2 tog, K16, K2 tog.
Next row: P.
Continue to dec at each end of K rows until 10 sts remain, ending on a P row. Cast off.

Right back
Rejoin yarn and complete as for left side, reversing shaping.

Head – all in one piece
Starting at front neck.
Cast on 14 sts.
First row: K6, inc in next 2 sts, K6.
Next row: P.
Next row: K7, inc in next 2 sts, K7.
Next row: P.
Continue to inc in this way until you have 22 sts, ending on a P row.
Next row: K9, K2 tog twice, K9.
Next row: P.
Next row: K8, K2 tog twice, K8.
Next row: P.
Mark each end of last row.
Next row: K2 tog, K5, K2 tog twice, K5 K2 tog.

Next row: P.
Next row: K2 tog, K3, K2 tog twice, K3, K2 tog.
Next row: P.
Next row: K2 tog at each end of row (8 sts).
Next row: P.
Next row: Inc 1, K to last 2 sts, inc 1, K1.
Next row: P.
Rep last 2 rows twice (14 st).
Mark each end of last row.
St st 8 rows straight.
Dec 1 st at each end of next and foll. alt row.
Next row: P.
Cast off.

Ears – make 2 pieces

Cast on 7 sts.
Starting with a P row, st st 3 rows.
Next row: K2 tog at each end of next and foll. alt row (3 sts).
Next row: Inc purlwise in first 2 sts, P1.
Next row: Inc 1, K2, inc 1, K1 (7 sts).
St st 3 rows.
Cast off.

Arms – make 2

Cast on 5 sts.
First row: Inc in every st (10 sts).
Next row: P.
Next row: Inc 1, K to last 2 sts, inc 1, K1.
St st 7 rows.
Next row: Inc 1, K to last 2 sts, inc 1, K1 (14 sts).
St st 5 rows. Mark each end of row.

To shape top of arms
Next row: K2 tog at each end of row.
Next row: P.
Rep last 2 rows until 4 sts remain.
Cast off.

To make up

Sew up all pieces with right sides together unless otherwise stated.

Arms

Fold each arm lengthways and sew up to markers. Turn right side out.

Body

Fold teddy so that the seam lies at the back and sew up legs, bottom and back, leaving a gap at centre back to make stuffing easier. Insert arms and sew up raglan seams.

Ears

Fold ears and sew up side seams. Turn right side out and oversew bottom edges.

Head

With right sides tog, fold head and sew side seams from neck to markers. The gaps left are for inserting the ears. Carefully fit the bottom edge of ears into the gaps, lining up all the edges and sew firmly through all layers.

Turn head right side out and stuff. Sew head to body, pushing more stuffing into the neck as you go. Tie a length of yarn around neck, tighten slightly and sew ends into the body out of sight.

Stuff legs and body firmly except around the tops of the legs and at raglan arm seams where there should be less to allow for easier movement. To further help teddy to sit, sew a small running st diagonally from the crutch to the hips through all layers.

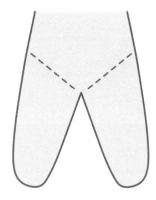

Face

With 3 strands of brown embroidery thread, embroider the features. (For sewing the eyes you could refer to the mini dolls faces as a guide).

Harriet's Clothes

Pyjama Top

Front

With 3mm needles and white yarn, cast on 24 sts and work in K1, P1 rib for 2 rows. Change to 3¼mm needles and lilac. Starting with a K row, st st 8 rows *.

To shape armhole

Cast off 2 sts at the beg of next 2 rows. K2 tog at each end of next and every alt row until 14 sts, ending on a P row.

To shape left front

Next row: K2 tog, K4, turn and work on these sts only for now.
Next row: P.
Next row: K2 tog at each end of row.
Next row: P.
Next row: K2 tog, K1.
Next row: P2 tog and fasten off.

Right front

With right side facing leave next 2 sts on a safety pin, K to last 2 sts, K2 tog.
Complete as for left front, reversing shaping.

Back

Work as front until *.

To shape armholes and back opening.

Next row: Cast off 2 sts, K until there are 10 sts on right hand needle, turn.
Next row: K2, P to end.
Next row: K2 tog, K to end.
Next row: K2, P to end.
Rep last 2 rows until 5 sts remain.
Leave sts on a safety pin for now.

With right side facing, rejoin yarn, Cast on 2 sts at beg of row, K to end.
Next row: Cast off 2 sts, P to last 2 sts, K2.
Next row: K to last 2 sts, K2 tog.
Next row: P to last 2 sts, K2.
Rep last 2 rows until 7 sts.
Leave sts on a holder for now.

Sleeves – make 2

With 3mm needles and lilac yarn, cast on 18 sts and work in K1, P1, rib for 2 rows. Change to 3¼mm needles and White *.
Next row: Inc 1, K to last 2 sts, inc 1, K1.
Next row: P.

To shape armholes

Cast off 2 sts at beg of next 2 rows.
Dec 1 st at each end of next and every foll. alt row until 6 sts remain, ending on a P row.
Leave sts on holder for now.

Neck

Join raglan seams.
With right side facing, 3mm needles and white yarn, K across the 7 sts of left back, 6 sts of left sleeve, pick up and K 4 sts along left front, K2 from holder, pick up and K 4 sts along right front, 6 sts of right sleeve and 5 sts of right back (34 sts).
Rib 1 row. Cast off in rib.
Sew up remaining underarm seams.
Neaten back opening with a couple of sts and sew on a press fastener.

Pyjama trousers – make 2 pieces

Starting at ankle, with 3mm needles and lilac yarn, cast on 26 sts and work in K1, P1 rib for 2 rows.
Change to 3¼mm needles and white yarn. St st 14 rows, ending on a P row.

To shape crutch

Cast off 2 sts at beg of next 2 rows.
Continue in st st for 12 more rows, ending on a P row *.
Next row: K4, (K2 tog, K4) to end.
Change back to 3mm needles and work 2 rows in rib. Cast off in rib.

To make up

With right sides together, fold each leg in half lengthways and sew up leg seam.
Turn one leg right way out and fit this one inside the other. Sew up crutch seam and turn right side out.

Dungarees

First leg

With denim, work as for pyjama trousers's up to *.

Leave sts on a spare needle for now.

Second leg

Work as for first leg to *.

** Next row: K to end of row and then across first 10 sts of first leg, turn and K20, turn and leave all remaining sts on a safety pin for now.

Back of bib

Next row: K1, K2 tog, K to last 3 sts, K2 tog, K1.

Next row: K1, P to last st, K1.

Continue to dec in this way until 10 sts remain, ending on a K row.

Next row: K3, cast off next 4 sts, K to end. You should have 2 sets of 3 sts each for the straps.

Working in g. st, K 20 rows for each strap and cast off.

Front

With right side facing, rejoin yarn and K across sts of left and then right leg (24 sts).

Next row: K.

Next row: K1, K2 tog, K to last 3 sts, K2 tog, K1.

Next row: K1, P to last st, K1.

Continue to dec in this way until 10 sts remain, ending on a K row.

Next row: K.

Cast off.

Fold and sew up inside leg seams then crutch seam. Sew press fasteners to ends of straps and on front bib.

Pocket

Cast on 6 sts and P 1 row.

Next row: Inc 1, K to last 2 sts, inc 1, K1.

St st 4 rows, ending on a K row.

Cast off and sew to front bib.

Roll neck sweater

Front and back pieces alike

Using soft yellow yarn throughout, work as for front of pyjama top to start of armhole shaping.

To shape armhole

Cast off 2 sts at the beg of next 2 rows. Dec 1 st a t each end of next and every alt row until 10 sts remain, ending on a P row.

Leave sts on a holder for now.

Make a second piece.

Sleeves – make 2

Work as for pyjama sleeves to *.

St st 2 rows.

Next row: Inc 1, K to last 2 sts, inc 1, K1.

St st 3 rows.

Complete as for pyjama sleeves from 'To shape armholes' (6 sts).

Neck

With right side facing, join 3 of the raglan seams. Starting at edge of remaining open seam, K across all sets of sts. Work in K1, P1 rib for 7 rows. Cast off in rib. Sew up remaining seam.

Day Bed

I have used 4mm needles for the bed base to speed things up a bit as it is quite a long piece before folding, but the top cover looks neater knitted with smaller needles.

Base

With 4mm needles and cerise yarn, cast on 50 sts and work in st st until bed measures about 60cm (24 in).

Cast off.

Top

The top cover is knitted sideways. You will need to wind off a second small ball of light pink yarn to join in and continue after each 1 row of white and have 4 small lengths of white yarn, one for each row.

With 3¼mm needles and light pink yarn, cast on 40 sts

Starting with a K row, st st 10 rows.

Join in white and K 1 row.

Join in second ball of pink and starting with a P row, st st 9 rows.

Continue to K 1 white row every 10th row until 4 stripes have been made. St st 9 more rows, ending on a P row.

Break off pink and white and join in cerise. Work in g. st for 6 rows. Cast off.

White trim

With 3¼mm needles and white yarn, cast on 40 sts.

Join in cerise yarn and K 1 row, break off, rejoin white yarn and st st for 9 more rows. Cast off.

To make up

Base

With right sides tog, fold in cast on edge so that the bed part measures 22cm (8½ in) and fold in the cast off edge so that the pillow measures 8cm (3 in) and both cast on and cast off ends are meeting. Sew up both long sides from top to bottom, leaving the cast on/off edges open. Turn right way out.

Flatten around the seams with your fingers and thumb. Pin down cast on/off edges for now.

With cerise yarn, backstitch through both layers about 1½cm (½ in) in from the edge all around bed. Backstitch cast on (bed) edge to bottom of bed, leaving pillow open. Remove pins and stuff pillow part and then over sew closed (see diagram).

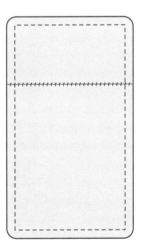

Top Cover

Have the top cover so that the wrong side is facing and pink edging is on the right hand side for now. Stripes should be vertical. With wrong side of white trim facing, pin and sew the cast off edge to the cover, using a small back st.

Turn your work over, fold the trim forward to the right side so that most of it is showing on the front (leaving about ½cm (¼ in) at the back so you cant see the join). Sew cast on edge to cover using small running st.

Lay the cover onto the bed with right side uppermost. Sew right hand side of cover to backstitch line on right hand side (as you look at it) of bed. Sew 3 press fasteners, evenly spaced, to left side of bed and the corresponding parts to wrong side of cover on g. st border.

Decorate the bed and pillow with felt hearts, using the templates as a guide if required and some 4mm white beads to the cover trim. Any sequins that you may have would also look pretty. I have also sewn a couple of daisy sts on the pillow (see diagram).

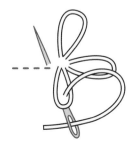

Baby's First Teddy

These little bears are made using the Harriet bear instructions, with a few small changes. One would make a very nice gift for a new born baby. There are no pieces that can be pulled off so are quite safe for young children.

Height
Approximately 18cm (7 in).

Materials
- Soft pink or blue DK baby yarn.
- Matching ribbon.
- 1 Pair 3mm knitting needles.
- Brown embroidery thread.
- Stuffing.

I wanted to use some good quality baby yarn for these bears so had to buy 50g balls. This is far too much for one bear but it can be saved for more bears later or passed on for someone else to make one.

Pink bear

Work as for the Harriet bear but with 2 rows less for first half of legs and 4 rows less for the back before armholes.

Blue bear

Unshaped feet.

First Leg

With blue yarn, cast on 8 sts.
First row: Inc knitwise in every st (16 sts). Starting with a P row, st st 11 rows.
Next row: Inc 1, K to last 2 sts, inc 1, K1. St st 7 rows. Leave on spare needle and make second leg.

Joining legs to body

Next row: K to last 2 sts, inc 1, K1, join in first leg thus: inc 1, K to end (38 sts). Continue body as for Harriet but work 4 rows less before armholes.

Work rest of bear as for Harriet.

Making up

Sew up and stuff the bears following the instructions for Harriet.

With 2 strands of brown embroidery thread and a sewing needle, embroider the features, making sure that the threads are extra securely fastened off as this bear will no doubt be chewed at some time. I have made 3 little claws on each paw but you may decide for safety to leave them off. I found some lovely pink and blue ribbon, with 'New Baby' embroidered through it, at a local craft shop. I should think there will be some in most wool and haberdashery outlets.

Brian

This little chap, based on the Harriet bear, comes already dressed. He is so quick to make up that lots of bears can be made, in many combinations of colours, for children in hospital, fundraising or as last minute Christmas gifts.

Height

Approximately 20cm (7¾ in).

Materials

- Oddments of DK yarn.
- 3mm knitting needles.
- Spare needle of similar size.
- Stuffing.
- Brown / Black embroidery thread.

Brian

Arms

Work as for Harriet bear, starting with head colour and changing to red yarn after 3 rows.
K 2 rows to make cuffs.
Starting with a K row, st st 4 rows.
Complete as for Harriet bear, starting with the inc each end of row but leave sts on a holder for now.

Legs

With brown, cast on 8 sts.
First row: Inc knitwise in every st (16 sts).
Starting with P, st st 5 rows. Break off brown.
Join in blue and K 2 rows.
Starting K, st st 8 rows.
Next row: Inc 1, K to last 2 sts, inc 1, K1.
St st a further 7 rows.
Leave sts on a spare needle and make second leg the same.
Next row: Inc 1, K to last 2 sts, inc 1, K1, K across sts of first leg thus:
Inc 1, K until last 2 sts, inc 1, K1 (40 sts).
Starting with a P row, st st 7 rows.
Leave sts on a spare needle for now.

Body

With red yarn, cast on 40 sts and rib 2 rows.

Join Jumper welt to trousers.
Hold the needle with red stitches in front of and adjacent to the spare needle with blue sts and knit 1 st from each needle at the same time.
Starting with a P row, st st 5 rows.
Complete as for Harriet bear from *

(to shape left back) but leave sts on a holder for now instead of casting off. Join all raglan seams in correct order, transferring all neck sts onto one needle with right side facing (28 sts).

Collar

Starting with a K row, rib 6 rows.
Cast off in rib.

Head and Ears

As for Harriet.

After stuffing, sew head to bear at the inside base of the collar, rolling it back out of the way for now. Sew seam of jumper welt separately from body when joining back seam.

Acknowledgements

I would like to say a big thank you to the following people who gave me such help and support with this book.

To my friends and family for their encouragement and advice. Especially to my friend Carrol Bates for all the proofreading and knitting up of so many little characters and their clothes. Also for being my friend when I needed one.

Thank you also to my mother Maureen Hassell and my friend Joy Walden for their support and for patiently listening to my endless monologue of ideas, yarn colours and body shapes.

Well done Jack Hartley, my gorgeous Grandson for trying to help me knit, very good for a three year old but we just need a bit more practise.

There isn't too much to thank my little dog Oscar for really. Running off with the wool and trying to eat the stuffing wasn't a great deal of help.

Thank you so much to all the lovely shop owners, customers and knitters for their ideas and encouragement and sending me their best wishes for the success of this book.

Of course there would not be a book without Gavin and Susan Crawford so thank you both for agreeing to publish my patterns and for all your hard work, skill and dedication in making such a lovely presentation of my toys.

About the Author

Sandra Polley has always enjoyed craftwork, especially knitting. She particularly enjoys creating little characters from scraps of yarn and her first book 'The Knitted Teddy Bear' was published in 2004.

Her designs have been featured in craft and knitting magazines, such as Simply Knitting and Woman's Weekly.

She also runs a successful small business 'Knits and Pieces' selling her patterns through yarn shops and companies throughout the UK.

Sandra now lives in Leicestershire and has two daughters, a young grandson and a very naughty little Border Terrier called Oscar.